HAVE PEN, WILL TRAVEL

BY THE SAME AUTHOR

M.J. Akbar	*India: The Siege Within*
M.J. Akbar	*Kashmir: Behind the Vale*
M.J. Akbar	*The Shade of Swords*
M.J. Akbar	*Kashmir: Behind the Vale*
M.J. Akbar	*Nehru: The Making of India*
M.J. Akbar	*Riot After Riot*
M.J. Akbar	*Byline*
M.J. Akbar	*Blood Brothers: A Family Saga*

OTHER LOTUS TITLES

Ajit Bhattacharjea	*Sheikh Mohammad Abdullah: Tragic Hero of Kashmir*
Amarinder Singh	*The Last Sunset: The Rise and Fall of Lahore Durbar*
Alam Srinivas & TR Vivek	*IPL: The Inside Story*
Ashok Mitra	*The Starkness of It*
LS Rathore	*The Regal Patriot: Maharaja Ganga Singh of Bikaner*
MB Naqvi	*Pakistan at Knife's Edge*
Maj. Gen. Ian Cardozo	*Param Vir: Our Heroes in Battle*
Maj. Gen. Ian Cardozo	*The Sinking of INS Khukri: What Happened in 1971*
Madhu Trehan	*Tehelka as Metaphor*
Mushirul Hasan	*India Partitioned. 2 Vols*
Mushirul Hasan	*John Company to the Republic*
Nayantara Sahgal (ed.)	*Before Freedom: Nehru's Letters to His Sister*
Peter Church	*Added Value: The Life Stories of Indian Business Leaders*
Sharmishta Gooptu and Boria Majumdar (eds)	*Revisiting 1857: Myth, Memory, History*
Shashi Tharoor & Shaharyar M. Khan	*Shadows Across the Playing Field*
Shrabani Basu	*Spy Princess: The Life of Noor Inayat Khan*
Shyam Bhatia	*Goodbye Shahzadi: A Political Biography*
Sunil Gupta	*Living on the Adge at Jhande Walan Thompson*
Susan Visvanathan	*The Children of Nature: The Life and Legacy of Ramana Maharshi*
Vir Sanghvi	*Men of Steel*
Zubin Mehta	*The Score of My Life*

FORTHCOMING TITLES

Michel De Grece	*The Raja of Bourbon*
SB Misra as told to Neelesh Misra	*The Story of an Ordinary Indian*

HAVE PEN, WILL TRAVEL

Observations of a Globetrotter

M.J. Akbar

LOTUS COLLECTION
ROLI BOOKS

Lotus Collection

First published in 2011
Second impression 2011
The Lotus Collection
An imprint of
Roli Books Pvt. Ltd
M-75, Greater Kailash II Market, New Delhi 110 048
Phone: ++91 (011) 4068 2000
Fax: ++91 (011) 2921 7185
E-mail: info@rolibooks.com
Website: www.rolibooks.com
Also at Bangalore, Chennai, Jaipur, Mumbai & Varanasi

Layout: Naresh L Mondal
Cover Caricature: Sandeep Adhwaryu

ISBN: 978-81-7436-815-7

Typeset in Perpetua by Roli Books Pvt. Ltd.
and printed at Rakmo Press, New Delhi.

To Khushwant Singh,
the Master

CONTENTS

CHILDREN OF THE MOTHER COUNTRY

WILD WEST MILD WEST

MEXED MISSAGES

FACES OF THE MOON

ACKNOWLEDGEMENTS

HAVE YOU EVER WONDERED why 'list' is the last syllable of 'journalist'? Because the list of those who need to be thanked is as important as a journalist. Truth to tell, the former does not exist without the latter.

Between the known, the remembered, the evident and the forgotten, the number of people who have helped in big and small ways is countless. A travelogue is theatre without starring leads, but full of exciting, brilliant visceral small parts adding up to a wonderful whole. There is no value judgement involved in the sense of who was more helpful or less; every bit of help is equally important. This provides me with the perfect copout, attached with an apology: sorry, if I cannot thank everyone individually. But I am particularly grateful to one institution and one individual. Without the Red Cross the extraordinary visit to Mogadishu, Somalia and Ogaden would have been impossible. And without Joyeeta Basu's editing, this book would have had an additional chapter with the saddest title in publishing: 'Errata'.

INTRODUCTION

THE ROAD IS A CLICHÉ, but not a lie. You meet an endless host of strangers along any journey, lives slipping in and out of events, not necessarily propelled by consistency or logic. Facts are not the only friends you make on the road. Far more interesting might be the paradox that awaits you in a teashop, or the anomaly that guides you towards an unexpected destination. The best experience is often like a blind date, but only if your mind is empty of both prejudice and preference.

You must travel light to get anywhere, and the heaviest baggage could easily be the preconceived notion. The fascination of a blind date is that it opens your eyes to the multiple dimensions of the possible. Prejudice is a blindfold, and darkness can only be the living room of phantoms, not the open space of reality.

Is reality too difficult a word, perhaps even a pompous claim in the limited armoury of a reporter? The traveller's knowledge cannot extend beyond what the eye can see, or the mind enquire, within the squeezed limits of time available. These qualifications necessarily invite the contempt of those who devote a lifetime to specialization within a narrow band. But we all live within brackets. As a journalist one might be occasionally right and often wrong, but that matters less than the definitive criterion: we must be honest. If the pen writes it as it sees it, without the compromise and temptation that can so easily corrupt the ink, it is enough, it will serve.

The most alluring temptation is certainty. I find it entirely appropriate that convict and conviction share the same root. Those who are too certain become prisoners of the known, unable to expand their vision towards the fascinating curlicues of the unknown. Time can be a merciless enemy of conventional wisdom. I hope you are surprised, or even shocked, by the fact that in the 1930s scientists advised girls to eat cake to lower their urge for sex. Who knows what will be made of today's 'truth' in 2080. Do not for a moment believe that scientists are immune from the influenza of absurdity. Marie Stopes, who gave us birth control and safe abortion [thank you, Marie], studied genetics because she was worried about the 'decline' in the genes of the great British race whose genius had created the world's greatest empire. She also disowned her son because he wanted to marry a girl who wore spectacles. Ogden Nash, I think, noted that men don't make passes at girls who wear glasses. This had little to do with beauty; eyes can improve within frames. Maybe those men were disciples of Marie, and bad eyesight denoted a defect in genes, and therefore would affect the genetic purity of the next generation. Perhaps you can now understand why Europe travelled from the 1930s into the 1940s.

A passing tip for penrakers: information is almost never useless. Store it away, like the most fastidious squirrel, in some corner of the mind, and then take out insurance by putting it in a notebook. You never know when it might become relevant. Who can predict when Marie Stopes and Ogden Nash will co-exist in the same paragraph.

A parting tip for penrakers on the road: the pen and the camera are not rational partners. The camera is not a supplementary tool or an evidentiary asset. It is either its own weapon, or it is useless. The best photograph can turn a moment into a metaphor. The writer's job is to link thousands of moments into a great narrative. That is our job: to tell the story. For reasons too complicated for this little bit of introspection, the word 'story' has been dragged into the nebulous zone between art and artifice. But the greatest stories ever written are eyewitness accounts of epic events, in which the quality of vision and command of the inner music of words elevates fact to the high ground of art. The best journalism has less lofty ambitions, but can give as much pleasure without getting entangled into the more serious business of offering instruction. Trust the eye, be a great witness, and the journey is soon touched by the magic of that truly exotic creature called the human being.

M.J. Akbar
Delhi

The Continent of Light

1

11 JANUARY 2006
IN THE NAME OF THE WARLORD

MOGADISHU, SOMALIA: ON 2 December 2005, His Excellency Eng. Hussein Mohammad Farah Aideed, Deputy Prime Minister (politics and security), Minister of Interior, Transitional Federal Government of the Somali Republice, called by appointment on India's High Commissioner in Nairobi Surendra Kumar. He was dressed in a dark blue suit, tie and leather-strap sandals. The 'Eng.' before his name was similar to 'Dr': Engineers now like to be known that they are thus qualified. In Somalia the preferred title of Hussein Aideed is 'General', a claim by hereditary right.

His father General Mohammad Farah Aideed became the world's most famous warlord, immortal in local lore and deified by Hollywood when, in 1993, he broke American will by downing two Black Hawk helicopters and killing 18 American Marines whose bodies were dragged through the streets of Mogadishu, capital of Somalia. A reward of a million dollars was placed on his head and he was nicknamed, for some obscure reason, Yogi the Bear. The father did not die in an American prison, but in his own city. His son was living in America and had trained to become a reserve Marine. When his father died, he returned to Somalia to inherit the title and the loyalty of his father's militia, though not the respect that his father commanded. Neither father nor son believed that the term 'warlord' was appropriate. Aideed means 'one who rejects insults'.

He seemed sincere, said Surendra Kumar. Hussein Aideed promised peace would finally come to Somalia in about six months, thanks to the latest deal brokered by mostly well-meaning (or simply fed-up) neighbours. He asked for Indian assistance in de-mining southern Somalia, building roads, improving healthcare and training the police.

Uniforms and guns for the police would not be unwelcome. Since there is nothing called a police force in Somalia at the moment, perhaps Hussein Aideed wanted arms and training for his own force. Kumar was diplomatic in his response; the visitor's charm was not sufficient to reduce the host's scepticism. The news is that India is not in any hurry to arm and train anyone or rebuild roads which are controlled by AK-47-wielding bands who laugh as they collect their tax from any vehicle brave enough, or desperate enough, to travel. The government of Hussein Aideed used to be based in Nairobi until the Kenyans exhausted their patience and told them to go.

Somalia is not a country in search of a government. It is a government in search of a country.

FROM THE AIR, MOGADISHU is entrancing, lean and stretched out against the Indian Ocean, a city of two million in a country of seven. It begins in the greenery of banana trees in the south, curves along the pristine beaches untouched by the large waves that break much before the shore. The city ends where the sand rises to cliff height in the north before spreading into the arid and endless desert.

We flew into an airport in the north in a Red Cross plane. The Red Cross is now the only international organisation with a national presence in Somalia, working to bring a touch of contemporary concern to a land that has been driven back into a pre-industrial past by criminal greed and mindless violence.

The breeze cools the midday sunshine and throws sand into our eyes. The airport was built by Osman Hassan Ali Atto, warlord and politician, to ferry *khat*, a local nerve-soother. When the international airport closed down, its fortunes boomed. Wisely, Atto decided to share such fortunes with a fellow warlord. The commerce is limited but it is a commercial hub of sorts.

In 1998, two Red Cross officials disembarked at this airport from a similar plane and wandered off to answer a call of nature behind a nearby sand dune, a reasonable need after a two-and-a-half-hour flight. They were lucky. The rest of the group was kidnapped by gunmen who appeared over a small hill and held hostage for ten days. Somalia is now one of two regions where the Red Cross uses armed guards, rather than the humanitarian credibility that keeps it safe elsewhere. The only other place is Chechnya.

There are three structures at this airstrip, nearly indistinguishable from the colour of the surrounding desert. The first, about ten feet wide with a sloping tin roof, is both the cafeteria and the bank: you can get a soft drink while you change foreign exchange for Somali shillings. There was a time when a dollar fetched 30,000 shillings, but the rate has stabilised at 15,000.

Warlords print the Somali currency. There is an advertisement of a cellphone company on the second hut, which is possibly an office. The third structure on an airstrip devoid of any human habitation for miles is a mosque, an Ottoman crescent atop its minaret.

A small craft of Aviation Sans Frontiers is waiting to take off when we land: the two NGO planes constitute the business of the day. A man near the tarmac with a cap, a piece of cloth wrapped around both ears, a football-referee whistle in one hand and a *tasbeeh* (prayer beads) in the other is the air traffic clearance authority. Each item has a function.

The cap is for the sun. The cloth is for the sand. He keeps in touch with the pilot with the whistle and with God with the prayer beads.

Our plane is refuelled while we wait. Three skinny, industrious men, two of them in the trademark *lungi*, kick-roll dented drums from a Dyna 350 semi towards the plane. A wheelbarrow, carrying a hose and a small engine accompanies them. The drums contain the fuel. Each is opened, with some effort, by a metal strip that fits into a groove in the cap and twists the cap around. One end of the hose goes into the drum, the other into the plane. The engine is pulled into a gurgle. Oil begins to flow up.

They travel about a hundred metres or more ahead, obscured by a windscreen of powdery desert dust: nine men on the back of a powerful Toyota, their legs dangling over the side, each with an AK-47 of varying power and enough ammunition to start a small war. In the centre is a mounted heavy machine-gun, manned by a burly brother in a bandana, with don't-fool-with-me in his eyes and a pistol in his belt. In local parlance, they constitute a 'technical'. No self-respecting warlord travels with less than four 'technicals'. Since this one has been hired to protect us, I suppose this 'technical' is on the side of the angels but loyalties are variable in a cash-and-carry business.

We drive over sand and rock towards the world's largest, or perhaps only, ghost city. An occasional man sleeps under a desert shrub. Lonely men squat on the edge of the track, waiting for nothing, their faces drained of all expectation. Women, in rare ones or twos, are defined by the bright colours of their dress, principally a dramatic red interspersed by a soothing yellow. The rest is silence in a vast emptiness, broken only by the periodic and minimal radio exchanges between our SUV and our 'technical'.

Suddenly, to our left, appears a huge scrapyard, a crazy museum of twisted, shattered metal, carcasses of cars, machines, yesterday's homes, anything that could be pillaged. It is owned by Bashir Raghe, a warlord. A minute later we see a large ship sitting impassively offshore. This is the scrap metal trade, a lucrative byproduct of a destruction-economy and yet another fortune for warlords to kill over.

'Do you know where the scrap is headed?' asks a friend whom I shall leave unnamed.

I don't.

To India.

To the right, in another minute, is what seems to be a mirage: a pink villa from an Italian seashore. Who lives there? A businessman. What is his business? He owns a bone factory.

A destruction-economy has more than one byproduct.

So far, I note, I have seen seven beneficiaries of this economy: the warlords; Japanese vehicle manufacturers (all registrations in Dubai or Sharjah); the Russian armaments industry; Belgian pistol-makers; telecommunications equipment makers; shipowners and Indian scrap merchants. Add an eighth, I am told. Coca-Cola. There is a flourishing Coca-Cola factory in the south of the city. Life goes better with Coca-Cola, particularly amidst death.

THE FIRST SIGHT OF Mogadishu is unreal. It is like seeing ruins from the wrong end of time.

The jagged edges of Rome's or Amman's amphitheatre symbolise the achievements of 2,000 years ago. In Mogadishu, you see the ruins of a flourishing twentieth century city in an environment that has regressed 2,000 years. Only a few of the shell-shocked homes seem inhabited; strangely there is utter silence even among the sparse patches of life.

I am given a guided tour of devastation: here what was once an enclave of diplomatic homes or an embassy row during the era of the

Soviet-supported President Siad Barre, there nothing where once the Indian Embassy existed. Every hundred paces is dull repetition of what used to be. The true sadness of Mogadishu is not what it has become, but what it once was and what it could have been.

The radio crackles. We cannot go to the Italian cathedral built when they colonised this part of Somalia. The 'technical' has reported that a gunbattle is going on in front of the cathedral. And so, without any fuss, we turn left a little before the gunbattle and drive into what was once the pride of the city: the main street, full of banks, businesses, government offices, cars, pedestrians, restaurants, bars and hotels. The street ends at the embankment. A majestic hotel sweeps in a classic Italian curve to our left, architecture that once hummed to the music of hundreds of rooms. It has now been blasted apart, shattered by tank battles that destroyed this street and city.

We get off at the embankment, which is broken at one place leaving a large gap. One tank, unable to brake, crashed through at this point. The tank lies on the rocks of the ocean shore, rusted, its turret tilted up, still searching for an enemy of the same colour and blood. It is as distressing a memory as the Fascist pillar nearby that has survived on the promenade from the time of Mussolini.

We are at the Hammaruin. We change guard. Literally. Our gunmen are all smiles as they wave goodbye; their replacements smile more broadly as they welcome us. But they don't smile at one another.

This is the dividing line between the north and south of Mogadishu. Militia from the north cannot enter the south, and naturally vice versa. In the ocean, a handful of children chatter and skip over the rocks, the shallow water being their only entertainment. On the street, from a corner, young men with nothing to do but clutch triggers at their nerve-ends watch as we switch vehicles and guards. A gun is part of the normal dress code of normal young men.

Engineer Hussein Aideed, leader of the United Somali Congress-Somali National Alliance, is yet to reach middle age. His mother, Asli Dhubat, his father's first wife, took him to the United States as a teenager. He joined the US Marine Corps Reserves in 1987, became a corporal and told the Associated Press in Somalia, 'Once a Marine, always a Marine'. He has, he believes, a wonderful idea for Somalia's future.

There are no passports in Somalia; even Kenya does not recognise a warlord passport any more. Hussein Aideed told Surendra Kumar that he was negotiating with an Indian IT company to create e-passports. The cost was estimated at $25 million. He had worked it out. An account would be opened in a prestigious international bank; 80 per cent of the passport fee deposited in this account would go to pay for the initial cost and 20 per cent would be sent on to Somalia. This would eventually pay the $25 million.

It seems a great idea for California.

12 JANUARY 2006

BATTLE WOUNDS

MOGADISHU, SOMALIA: WHERE DO you find war? In a graveyard or a hospital. There are no stories in a graveyard. A hospital, on the other hand, has too many.

The director of Medina Hospital was in Mecca. It seemed the appropriate place for Sheikh Don to be. He had left for Dubai en route to Haj by the south city airport on a Russian Antonov. An extremely enterprising private airline ferries those who can afford the minimum fare of $250. There is even an occasional flight to Paris. Where there is a will there is a way. The south city airport, unlike its poor cousin in the north, is protected by anti-aircraft guns.

Medina Hospital was built by the Germans for the local police and has proper buildings, lovely trees in the spacious compounds, a high water reservoir and space for 500 beds. About 65 – always add a few for battle casualties – function now.

Our guide is Dr Ali the White, a jovial Somali who refuses to get depressed by his difficulties. Instead, he breaks into song when he learns that I am an Indian. Thankfully, it is not *Mera joota hai Japani,* but the rather surprising *Meri muhabbat jawan rahegi, sada rahi hai sada rahegi*. May I add that he got the tune right!

I am not brave enough to face another's pain and the visit to the wards was acutely discomforting. The relatives around each bed looked stoic as they fanned their loved child, or simply waited. There are few old men or women in hospital. That is the meaning of war.

The most important doctor is the chief surgeon, which tells the story. Dr Hassan Osman is legitimately proud that one of the techniques he has devised for immediate operations is now quoted in medical journals. The wounded come from as far away at Diinsoor, which is 500 kilometres away. That is reputation in a war zone.

The police disappeared from Medina in 1991, when the remnants of government crumbled. It was partially reopened in 1992 with the help of Medicins Sans Frontiers (Doctors without Borders). Patients were treated under trees. There was no water or power. A hospital is perhaps the only thing that brings clans together in wartime. The elders got together and contacted the Red Cross in 1999, which stepped into desolation. In 2000 a generator arrived, which purrs quietly in a large shed and turns Medina into an island unrecognisable from its environs: a full drugstore, surgical equipment, doctors who are taken to one annual conference, nurses and, perhaps most important, community involvement. It was the community that paid for the new tiles in one ward and painted the buildings.

If Medina is a marvel then Keysaney is a miracle. This hospital in the north was a prison outside the city, on the shore, making it, as someone wryly observed, the 'most secure hospital in the world'. When the Siad Barre regime collapsed the prison emptied.

Compared to Medina, the facilities are rudimentary. The strength of Dr Ahmed Muhammad Ahmed, a devout young man who prays five times a day, and his colleagues is inspiring. This is the only hospital for the north and has treated more than 55,000 patients in over a decade. Add more than 100,000 outpatients. The Red Cross turned this prison into a hospital in November 1991. There are four wards, including one for VIPs, which means it has curtains. Dr Ahmed showed me with shy pride the apparatus he had set up to recycle a bullet victim's blood back into the patient.

The one thing you can't get in a bloodstained country is blood.

The main hall at Keysaney doubles up as an English classroom for the staff in the evenings, thanks to Dr Ahmed. The sentences chalked on the blackboard are instructive in more ways than one. 'A: Do you think you can get me to Victoria by half-past? B: We should be OK if the lights are with us. A: You've still got five minutes to spare. A: Pounds 6.40 please.' The last sentence was: 'I go to a private institute which is called Oxford.'

You find both war and aspiration in Dr Ahmed's fly-blown hospital.

The unsentimental fortitude of doctors is remarkable. Dr Ahmed takes nothing for granted and everything in his stride. Dr C. Oscar Avogadri has just joined the Red Cross team for Somalia. He is an Italian who spent some time in Nepal but, much to his relief, did not understand cricket – otherwise, he might have spent eight hours on a weekend watching the game instead of doing something better. Pascal Hundt, head of the Somalia division, is Swiss, imperturbable, practical and measures a day by how much he has got done, whether stocking medical supplies or injecting capital into the rural economy by financing 5,000 goats or telling impoverished representatives of a betrayed people that he cannot change the rules. He is already planning for a famine that looms ahead.

THE PRICE OF WAR is poverty. Somalis do not have the individual or collective resources to fight a famine. The destitution is utter. Clothes are old, slippers tattered, food basic. There are no shops, apart from the occasional medical (what else?) store or a utility outlet. There is no state, and therefore no state service. Water and electricity must be purchased from entrepreneurs; travel rights from the gun-toting militias. The thin elite owns generators. For visitors with foreign exchange and a hotel room there is excellent fruit juice and lobster from the Indian Ocean. For the nomad, or the citizen, life hovers at subsistence level. Measure incomes on a simple scale. The best paid are top-of-the-line gunmen, who get a hundred dollars a month. Fifty dollars will fetch you a bullet-sprayer (a bullet costs 30 cents). Most of the gunmen don't have shoes either.

There may be no money for food, but there is always enough money for war.

My friend remembers this fact with a hint of awe: the only time the price of food collapsed was in 1991, when the Americans came, leading an international effort to fight famine and starvation, restore governance and leave behind a semblance of civil society. A 50-kg bag of rice that cost $450 during famine was available for nine dollars. (The current price is $50.)

So what was the mistake that the world's most powerful country made in the world's weakest country?

Cultural insensitivity is too boring an accusation. A diplomat who was in and out of Somalia at that time and lives in Nairobi has more relevant analysis. The Americans were not interested in peacekeeping; they wanted something that they called peace-building. They wanted an architecture that would stabilise the country around a democratic polity. It was another honourable intent, that came unglued when it hit the warlords. Every warlord was convinced that only he could become president of the Somali Republic. In a bid to challenge the lords,

American soldiers raided the home of the most powerful, Aideed. That was the end of both peacekeeping and peace-building. The American position on the country is: Somalia missed the bus a decade ago; it will not be given another chance.

There are others ready to take a chance or provide one. The last spot on our tour of Medina Hospital was the newly-painted canteen for families of patients, another stray sign of normalcy in an abnormal world. The doctors left me alone: clearly no one senior ever ventured into a public canteen. If they wanted coffee outside office they sat on benches in the shade of trees. Even Dr Ali the White left me. I wandered in. The painting was fresh; the walls sparkled with schoolchildren's paintings of the usual variety, animals, scenery et al. To my right, in a panel, were two highrise buildings. On top of one was a legend: New York. A similar masthead on the other was filled with black. Two airplanes were exploding against the upper stories of both buildings. In the space between the towers, in small lettering, was a phrase. Since I can read Arabic, I knew what it said. Al Qaeda.

Perhaps someone reading this will get into a pother and that painting, done by someone doing community service for the hospital in a canteen the senior staff did not enter, will be erased. That is not the point. The point is what is happening to the community in Mogadishu, living on the deserted, rubble-strewn streets around Medina.

I could not resist the question as I said goodbye to Dr Ali the White. Surely that could not be his real name. No. His name was Dr Ali Muallim. Then...? 'Oh,' he said with a big grin, 'white because I am so black. Just reverse!'

Just reverse. It seems a good metaphor for Mogadishu.

14 JANUARY 2006

FAITH FILLS VACUUM IN LAND OF CLANS

MOGADISHU, SOMALIA: FEAR IS RATIONAL. As long as one is anonymous, death can only be an accident. It is superfluous to fear an accident in a minefield: the mine has nothing personal against you. It became different when my friend said, while we were dining on the terrace of the Shamo Hotel and Residence Plaza, a heavenly breeze blowing from the Indian Ocean, the stars of the southern hemisphere dominated by

Mars to my left and the Orion belt to the right of my occasional gaze: 'This is an oral society.'

We were at the hotel where a few months ago Kate Peyton of the BBC had been shot dead.

So far, I felt far more protected by anonymity than the 'technicals'. The Red Cross does not advertise its travel plans. Unlike the United Nations (when it is around – it disappeared from Somalia in March 1995), which believes in the power of the press release, the Red Cross appreciates the virtues of silence. But by now word would have spread that a journalist was in tow: this is an oral society. A big boy might want to know why he had not been lined up for an interview. Press coverage is good for the self-esteem of a warlord trying very hard to look like a peacelord.

Kate Peyton made a number of mistakes. The crucial one was that she walked out of the single entrance-exit, across the compound and out of the gate to get into a car that was meant to take her to the Sahafi Hotel (Journalists' Hotel, so named in honour of the media flock that constituted its last crowd during the battles of 1993). Unlucky. A single shot, which is rarely fatal, got her. She was rushed to Medina Hospital but her moment had come.

Our technicals, as well as our Land Cruiser, are inside the compound. Everyone sleeps behind walls. Zakaria, the young waiter, speaks excellent English. The only other guest is a Chinese resident who is often on his cellphone: mobile phones are the most successful business in Somalia and any international call costs only 30 cents since there are no licence fees and very little advertising. A young and fair Arab is with him, perhaps his partner. In an adjoining room a radio sparkles to life and a tall waiter begins to dance with abandon, his tray twirling on his fingertips. From the roof, Mogadishu is peaceful, quiet and patchily lit. There are no mosquitoes. The ocean breeze has driven them away. The moon is seven nights old and the stars are unaffected by the gauze of industrial pollution. I switch on television in my room after dinner and am pleasantly surprised by B4Music. And so to bed listening to Rabbi Shergill in Mogadishu and up with Dev Anand and *Hare Rama Hare Krishna* and *Ishq tera garam masala*. Dawn always, and illogically, seems so much safer than night.

Ten warlords are the principal arbiters of Mogadishu, but they do not control the only guns on the street. The nippiest guns now belong to the Sharia courts, possibly because they are the youngest, perhaps because they are motivated by more than money.

The south of the city has twice the life of the north, which means what it means. The old fish market is still dead. The office buildings are still stark, wounded and empty. A donkey cart stands at the entrance of a lane, selling water. A battered Fiat, looking as old as Mussolini, chugs by: it is the first personal civilian vehicle I see and has no number plates. A choking and lonely jeep is sign of some public transport. Then appears the first traffic jam: a truck and two donkey carts struggling to negotiate the rubble in front of a vegetable market just after the mosque.

There is a loudspeaker on the minaret of the Shaikh al-Sufi mosque. As the name suggests, Islam was spread by Sufi mendicants and dervishes in Somalia. There is no hard line on Somali sand. Women, their heads covered in bright cloth, are a normal part of public life and show as little hesitation as men when they spread a cardboard sheet or cloth and offer namaz at the call of the muezzin. A sign outside the mosque shows the way to a madrasa, the largest in the city. A little later we are overtaken by a Toyota with three young men at the back. They race ahead, oblivious of the rubble or carts or even a technical like ours. 'Sharia police,' explains my friend.

Their sense of power is evident in their speed and the slight adolescent jeer in their eyes. They are too young to care. Older gunmen in technicals, with bullet belts slung across the shoulder and coursing down expanding bellies, take care to travel in large bands. They have something to care about: their salaried lives. Fifty dollars a month gets you a technical or a fake passport, probably Ugandan.

Colonel Abdullahi Yusuf, President of the Transitional Federal Government (TFG) since 14 October 2004, has often said that he is going to destroy 'Islamic terrorists' in Somalia. Col. Yusuf was part of the problem for so long that he has, by the consensus of neighbours and grudging acceptance of nominated members of Parliament, been made part of the solution in the hope that there will be one. But it took him five months to enter Somalia after he became president and then relocate the capital to Jowhar. His prime minister, Ali Muhammad Gedi, was greeted with bomb blasts that almost killed him when he tried to address a public rally in Mogadishu in May 2005. He returned to Nairobi a trifle hastily.

SHEIKH HASSAN DAHIR AWEYS' henna-streaked beard is familiar to anyone in Mogadishu, as are his calm, softly-delivered sermons.

He lives near his mosque and was the most prominent leader of the Ittehad Islamiya. Ever since Washington put this organisation on its terror list after 9/11, everyone prefers to be known as a former leader. His security includes a truck with an anti-aircraft gun, but I doubt if that would be sufficient protection if the CIA decided to pick him up. America has no official presence in Somalia, but an anti-terrorist task force of 2,000 is based in Djibouti, a Somali region in the north that was given separate independence because it was under French rule. (A parallel event in India would have made Pondicherry a separate nation.) Sheikh Aweys makes no effort to hide his conviction that Somalia can only be saved by a conversion into an Islamic state, that America has launched a war against Muslims all over the world and that the CIA has on its payroll Somali warlords who pass on information as well as kidnap any suspect on America's wanted list. It is popular belief that CIA agents regularly visit their employees in Mogadishu, arriving by secret aircraft. Sheikh Aweys believes that Col. Yusuf makes the noises he does in order to get Western support for his notional government.

The Islamic movement in Somalia predates the current troubles, said Dr Ahmed Mohammad Hassan, president of the Somali Red Crescent Society and old enough to have seen it all. We met in Nairobi, where he lives. The clergy was the first, he pointed out, to protest against the 'scientific socialism' of the pro-Soviet Siad Barre, in January 1975. Barre publicly executed 11 respected clerics in revenge.

The clans, principally an alliance between Ali Mahdi and Mohammad Aideed (who, incidentally, served as ambassador to New Delhi for five years), drove out Barre in January 1991 and then spent the next year killing each other in thousands in the battle of succession. That was when famine devastated hundreds of thousands of Somalis who wanted a government rather than a civil war.

Who fills the gaps left by a withered state?

The Muslim Brotherhood came to a famished people in 1991 through effective relief work across the length of a long country in places like Merca, Kismayo, Dobley, Lugh, Berbera and, of course, Mogadishu. In June 1992 they, along with Ittehad Islamiya, instigated an insurgency in Puntland, eventually defeated by the Yusuf clan. In mid-1994, a council for the implementation of Sharia law was created with Sheikh Sharif Muhidin as its chairman, in Mogadishu North. It was the first experience of law in a country that had become lawless and helpless and established a positive image of the clergy.

A clan's power over people emerges from its role as a provider of essential necessities of life: security (in times of crisis, even food security), kinship, justice and an economic net without too many holes. What happens when the credibility of such a powerful, traditional institution is savaged?

Over the last 15 years, this essential fact of Somali society has indulged in spectacular self-destruction. The mosque is perhaps the only institution that provides a community net, education, justice that is implemented and a growing revenue system that can create a safety net. The mosque was always the sole source of salvation in the afterlife for a deeply religious people. It has now become the predominant source of salvation in this life as well.

The future of both the clans and the mosque began when Siad Barre fled in January 1991. Only one of the two will find the horizon.

15 JANUARY 2006

GUNS AND WARLORDS

HARAR, SOMALIA: HOW MANY guns make a warlord? 25 technicals, so about 250 armed men with Russian AK-47s and Belgian pistols make you a lord and you can go up the hierarchy to viscount or marquis or earl or proper baron if you include a couple of anti-aircraft guns and artillery pieces. But there are no kings in Somalia. A top of the line AK-47 costs between $400 and $500; many of the weapons are below the line. I picked up one, while we were lunching off chunks of dry roast camel in a *dhaba*, lent to me by a young man in a shy smile and a *lungi*. It was heavy, a little less than ten kilograms. I gave it back after making appropriate noises, carefully avoiding even passing contact with the trigger. At a rough glance, my benefactor had about a million and a half Somali shillings worth of ammunition in his belts: a dollar fetches three bullets.

Three great symbols of modern civilisation are available in Somalia: the AK-47, Coca Cola and the mobile phone. Three mobile phone companies, Nationlink, TelecomSomalia and Hormut, ensure proper competition. An international call costs only 30 American cents.

They also double up as money-transfer operations and one of them (defunct after landing up in the suspect category) sent Washington into paroxysms after 9/11 with a word that previously did not exist in a western dictionary but was perfectly understood in much of Asia, *hawala*. Americans were in Somalia a decade before 9/11 but never picked up this word. Maybe that is why they never stayed. You have to understand Somalia to stay in Somalia.

War is a great boon to technology. A cruise liner defended itself against heavily armed Somali pirate boats in 2005 with the LRAD, Long Range Acoustic Device. It emits a sound from a long range that the human ear cannot tolerate and has proved a brilliant answer to pirate guns. So as long as pirates are human they can be driven. I am told that the device is being used in Iraq to disperse unwanted crowds. For more details on LRAD check Google. The Almighty, Omnipotent Google knows all.

Their present having been stolen, Somalis take comfort in the past. Ancient Egyptians imported cinnamon, frankincense, tortoise shells and 'slaves of a superior sort' from Somalia and conceded that Somali civilisation matched their own. If the Magi were kings from Africa, then it is at least plausible that the one carrying frankincense for the infant Jesus came from Somalia. Ibn Batuta, the thirteenth century Tunisian traveller who did not waste time on inconsequential places, found Maqdashaw a 'town of enormous size' where 'a single person ... eats as much as the whole company of us would eat ... and they are corpulent in the extreme'. The only parallel I can think of is a Kashmiri enjoying his *wazwan* in front of us mere mortals, but of course the Kashmiri is not corpulent. The waters of Chashm-e-Shahi keep him slim.

HOW MANY CLANS MAKE a nation? The Arabs found 39 when Mogadishu became one of their principal trading colonies in the tenth century. This was the breakdown: Mukri (12), Djidati (12), Akati (6), Ismaili (6) and Afifi (3). The Mukri, who also had a dynastic ulema, were in the ascendant when Ibn Batuta visited the port. The nation-state is a recent idea. Nomadic Somalis lived across a far wider region than their present borders, including Ethiopia and Kenya. European colonisation came only towards the end of the nineteenth century. The British came to the north because, as they put it, they wanted guaranteed meat supplies for their garrison in Aden. The Italians wanted the fruit groves of the south. The French were tempted, typically, by temptation and occupied Djibouti. The clans did not wait to be conquered. They took the easy way out and sold their rights, most often for less than $100. The treaties were remarkable for their three-point simplicity. Point 1: All rights are yours. Point 2: I get $70 or $100. Point 3: You have the last word in all disputes. Neighbours could hardly resist exploiting such weakness. In 1891 Emperor Menelik II, founder of modern Ethiopia, wrote to European powers: 'Ethiopia has been for 14 centuries a Christian island in a sea of pagans. If Powers at a distance come forward to partition Africa between them, I do not intend to remain an indifferent spectator.' He did not. He sent word to Amir Abdullahi, ruler of the historic city of Harar and pivotal to Muslim east Africa, to accept his suzerainty. The Amir, heir to a dynasty of 72 generations, sent presents and a helpful suggestion, that Menelik should accept Islam. Menelik promised to conquer Harar and turn the principal mosque into a church. The Medihane Alam Church, in front of the Galma Amir Abdullahi, or the old palace, is evidence that Menelik kept his word.

The mosque was converted but not the people. While Ethiopia proudly and correctly claimed to have become Christian at the time of Constantinople, lands like Kenya changed only during the wave of missionary activity that accompanied colonisation in the nineteenth century. As Jomo Kenyatta, first President of independent Kenya, famously said, 'When the missionaries came to Africa, they had the Bible in their hands and we had the lands... We closed our eyes to pray and when we opened them, we had the Bible in our hands and they had the lands...'

HARAR HAS THE FEEL of a city that has travelled a long way through history but now has nowhere left to go.

UNESCO has recognised Harar, about 450 kilometres east of Addis Ababa through land rich in the local addiction, *chat* (or *khat*), a mildly intoxicating but stimulating leaf that is chewed slowly, as a heritage city. There is some excitement among the educated elite that UNESCO may do more for Harar than all the rulers since the defeat of Amir Abdullahi at the battle of Chelenko in 1887. There is hope but not too much trust. As a sociologist who did his post-graduate studies at the Tata Institute of Social Sciences in Mumbai some twenty years ago told me over mercato in the lovely café in the courtyard of the city, 'We have been living too long on a diet of pledges.'

Little was done for the people, who are of Somali origin, but bitter wars were fought over them. In the seventies, Siad Barre of Somalia invaded Ethiopia to take back the Ogaden region, where Harar is. Talk that Ogaden possessed huge reserves of oil and gas might have encouraged the invasion. Siad Barre's tanks penetrated deep into the desert before they were defeated by Cuban soldiers who acted as mercenaries of the Soviet Union (Ethiopia had a Marxist-Leninist regime then, a fact that merely Socialist Siad Barre forgot). Hararis remember the Cubans as a wild lot, shooting donkeys playfully even after being told how valuable these pack animals were. A few Cuban faces in a traditional and conservative society are more evidence that 'liberators' make their own rules.

The elders, gradually losing their eminence as a new anger slowly seeps through the young, are resigned to stagnation and the eyes flicker with old zeal only when they dream that Menelik's church will once again become a mosque in their lifetime. The people, as elsewhere in Ethiopia, can be strikingly good-looking. The girls wear embroidered head scarves or, rarely, the hijab with jeans. The boys are in the ubiquitous football T-shirt. One bearded young man had EBAMA, San Jose, California, Badr 2004 written on his T-shirt. It stood for Ethiopian Bay Area Muslim Association. Had he lived in America, I asked. No, he said. Few leave Harar. Those who go send T-shirts along with cheques but do not return.

THE MANSION IN WHICH the Lion of Judah, Haile Selassie, was born is in the old city, called Jubal, and was built by an Indian. You walk down a narrow stone alley full of shops and tailors with Singer sewing machines. Indians, particularly Bohras from Mumbai, dominated commerce during Muslim rule in Harar. Haile Selassie was born here because his father, Menelik's brother, was made governor after the defeat of Amir Abdullahi. UNESCO has allocated funds for the restoration of the mansion but ten families have made it their home and will not move. The most interesting occupant is a healer.

He sits, erect, on a mattress in a spacious drawing room on the ground floor. His fame is recorded for posterity in a notebook where his literate patients describe their miraculous recovery and attach passport-size photographs to add a face to their identity. He is 52 and learnt his skills from his father, whose picture is framed on the high wall behind him, above a carpet with a drawing of the holy mosque at Kaaba and a much-extended string of prayer beads which he uses for *dhikr*, a Sufi form of devotion, at night. A woman enters, kisses his extended hand twice while he continues talking to us and joins another with a child in a corner. There is a telephone on a table and two small tape-players, one broken. The telephone rings once during our visit and is picked by an aide lounging on the side who, we realise later, also speaks English. A notice board indicates that the healer cures all the tough diseases, including gynaecological problems, but, alas, back pain is not on the list. He assures me that he can repair nerves that wrack your back as well and there have been a cancer patient or two who has gone home happy. He explains that he uses herbs and plants and not shaman-style magic. Perhaps he tells villagers, who crowd around him in the mornings since they have to return by nightfall, something different; perhaps he is equally candid with them. He asks about herbal medicines in India and I include Tibet's fame in my response.

The notice outside affirms that the healer does not accept fees but donations for the cause are not unwelcome. I do not use his expertise but my donation is not unwelcome either.

2

20 OCTOBER 1996

KENYA DIARY: WAS BOB A SPELLING MISTAKE?

On our first night in Africa we swept through the local cuisine from A to Z: from Alligator to Zebra, with letters like O for Ostrich thrown in to keep the menu moving. Tip: leave space for zebra, particularly when cooked with the finesse of an African chief. The entertainment for the evening was provided by Helen doing a belly-swirl from *Inteqaam:* after an hour of 'tribal dancing' one could no longer be sure whether Hindi films had been influenced by Africa or reverse colonisation had won out. The trouble with our inaugural hotel, on the edge of Nairobi and advertised as the gateway to our magic tour, was that it was trying too hard to be ethnic. Even the name, Safari Hotel, was fake: the real safari would come later, where you could watch animals doing amazing things like sleeping, eating and protecting their young. Irony aside, Kenya is a lovely holiday, even if the entrance is through a tourist trap. Our first stop was a journey to the centre of the earth.

UnitedTouring Company (by far the best in the business) promised, but did not guarantee, heat and dust at Nanyuki. Our guide was doing his best to live up to the traditional image of Africa. Instead, this little outpost 6,389 feet above the sea was cool and breezy, with herds of cloud roaming the sky uncertain about whether to disperse into rain. A young man took charge of us. He undertook to provide scientific evidence of the passage of the Equator at this spot by taking a bowl of water (with a hole at the bottom) and making a matchstick twirl in the anti-clockwise direction 20 paces north of the Equator, and in the clockwise direction 20 paces south of the line. Or was it the other way around? The only thing one is certain about is that at the Equator the matchstick was obstinately still. The young man used a term to explain the phenomenon but he could not pronounce the word and we could not understand it. However, we did obediently pay four dollars each for a piece of paper certifying our presence at the hallowed spot.

The entertainment over, the group got down to the serious part of the visit to Nanyuki: a highly traditional African ritual called shopping for beads. I concocted other matters, like watching one of our drivers chat up his girlfriend who was braiding her mother's hair in the flirtatious sunshine. A sprightly lady came up and suggested that I absolutely must visit her shop: Bob's Stores. The name was printed boldly across the T-shirt. To reinforce her message, she pointed a finger to the sign on her breast touching first the B on her right nipple and then the S on the left nipple, with a smile on her face which suggested that whatever Bob might be selling at his Store, it wasn't antiques. On the other hand, could Bob have been a spelling mistake?

HOLLYWOOD, AS USUAL, HAD an even better idea what to do with the Equator. Why make only four dollars per visit when you could make four hundred?

In 1959, the great all-American hero William Holden, with the help of other big-game hunting friends like Ernest Hemingway, built what is surely the most magnificent club in the world: Mount Kenya Safari Club. On a height of 8,000 feet, it sprawls across a manicured, green landscape of lawns and trees, with the majestic Mount Kenya straight ahead and the Equator passing diagonally across its magnificent environment. Having been conceived in Hollywood, the club naturally insists on being British at dinner time. Although black tie is no longer de rigueur, smart casual (translation: no jeans) is a must. However, for the rest of the day you can chat with storks, have scones with tea in the lounge, savour the cricket-interrupted silence of the forests in the evening or simply sink in the power of the gods on those twin peaks above the clouds.

Like any god, Mount Kenya has many faces. Uniquely, it does not belong to any contiguous range, but slopes slowly above the plateau till at the centre, towering above the shoulders on either side, rises the rock of the mount, imperiously indifferent to the world at its feet. You can circle Mount Kenya by road and see a new dimension at every curve. From the Safari Club, at the level of the necklace of clouds around its neck, you bow in obeisance as the snow glitters on the crevasses at the touch of the morning sun. Alas: time melts. We have to leave – just before the temptation becomes irresistible to address dead celebrities on first-name terms: Bill and Papa. We shall return.

THE PRINCIPAL WORRY OF any prime mover on a safari holiday is that some jaundiced member of the party will look at the dollar hotel bill and mutter 'Ranthambore was better'. That particular problem had been more than solved by the third day, at the Samburu Serena Lodge, 3,000 feet up in the mountains of northern Kenya.

Mount Kenya was out of the normal world; Samburu was quintessential Africa. A lazy river ambled on its way down in front of our verandah, carrying the dust of the desert and scrublands beyond the mountains. An official warning stood sternly posted before our cabins and it had nothing to do with the leopard which came across most evenings to dine on the leg of mutton placed as a daily temptation on the far bank. A few years ago apparently the leopard acquired the habit of over-extending its welcome by swimming across the river to mingle with the guests. That has been stopped. The real danger is now from the monkeys on the trees outside our rooms: apparently they bite, or scratch, the hand that feeds them. More evidence that man has descended from monkeys.

The evening game drive was our first genuine safari. The bad news is that the lions really do stretch out and sleep, their postures the very emblems of laziness, exactly like Hobbes in the cartoon strip. The first three we saw treated our swarm of jeeps precisely as they treated the flies crowding on their bodies: with indifference, even when we were three or four feet away. Eventually we got tired of their somnolence; they did not wake up. But then appeared a lioness on the prowl, hunting for supper. Taut, quiet, patient as she stalked her prey, her concentration leaving no space for the swarm of cameras stuck to static eyes filming her every move. One began to feel a little irritated with oneself, as if we had turned the park into a jungle with our invasive intrusion. There was a literal traffic jam of vehicles as word spread that the big cats had been spotted. Perhaps the lioness got irritated, for she suddenly turned and streaked away leaving both her quarry and her predators behind.

The high point of our game drives came later, at the southern border of Kenya, in the reserve that stretches from the Masai Mara into the Serengeti National Park in Tanzania. It was seven in the morning, with the sun to our left and a wind blowing across from east to northwest. Our jeep edged up yet another hill, our binoculars scanning the horizon for something other than the plum-bum zebra or the jar-necked gazelle or the audacious dik-dik (a foot high antelope). Then suddenly appeared three lionesses: bright and immobile, about a hundred yards separating each of them from the other, in a straight line. A minute or two later, about 300 yards to our right, appeared a fourth lioness: flat on her belly, but equally alert, tense and still. All four were stalking two zebras in the distance. The zebras could sense hostility, but were unsure: their heads would rise to sniff the air for telltale smells or to glimpse the enemy. The two lionesses on either side of the strategic line would wait for each sign of complacency, then creep a little forward, not willing to move until they were certain that they would not be seen. It was the fourth lioness to our right who (perhaps literally) gave the game away; one by one the four cats sauntered across to the tip of the grassy mound to our left, began playing with one another, nuzzling, accepting failure in a spirit of friendship, and then lying down to return to their favourite occupation: sleep.

THE WILDEST WILD LIFE we encountered all week were American tourists. This was a bit of an upmarket trip: no backpackers please; ladies and gentlemen from Oklahoma and Osaka very welcome. The Americans were unrestrained in their oohs and aahs, their highest signal of admiration being expressed in the more terse 'gee whizzzz!' It was impossible not to learn detailed descriptions of their experiences at the exquisite Lake Naivasa Country Club, less than a 100 kilometres away from Nairobi but many lifetimes away in spirit. The huge lake is 6,800 feet above the sea. The hotel on its edge is classic colonial, out of the instruction book of Cecil Rhodes who told his architect to achieve 'the subordination of ornament to a single idea ... (acquire) breadth, simplicity, symmetry'. Enter two Americans, a gentleman and a lady.

'I am hot,' he said, 'I am the one who spotted the leopard.'

'Gee,' she said, 'I've seen everything except a leopard.'

'Awww, I only got a glimpse.'

'Ohhh.'

'Just a glimpse, sort of came as a cue.' He was genuinely apologetic by now.

'Oh! My cheetah looked at me!'

Enter third American. 'I just can't believe this. I put my head on the pillow and go to sleep. I got earmuffs for the night. Then what are we doing today?'

'You're going on a balloon. The others are going on a game drive.'

'Hell, noooo; whyyy?'

'You're doing only what others are doing, only you are doing it from the air.'

That was one explanation for spending 350 dollars on a hot-air ride.

Tailpiece: Why do they call this balloon ride across a game reserve a once-in-a-lifetime experience?

Because at that price no fool is going to do it again.

JAMAL, OUR TRAVEL AGENT, was charming on the telephone. 'The pilot will have your tickets.'

I believed him. The pilot came with my name on the manifest and a 19-seater that landed near a wind indicator and asked me to hop in. Two more stops on the Masai Mara to pick up passengers and then we would head for Nairobi. Sorry, folks, no smoking, no eating, no talking, no fighting, just grab those mints if there are any left.

One of the passengers, from America of course, got into the spirit of things. 'You're flying me to Chicago?' he asked.

'No,' replied the pilot. 'Too many wild animals in Chicago.'

3

15 DECEMBER 1996

A BIHARI IN MAURITIUS FINDS LIFE WITHOUT LALU

APOLOGIES FOR AN AUTOBIOGRAPHICAL note but the urge becomes irresistible when you land in a city built by your forefathers and named Plaisance. In the 1860s my eleven-year-old grandfather was driven out of a small village in Chapra district of Bihar, till then the complete circle of his horizon, by the unforgiving fact of hunger. Destiny took him to a teashop in a slum 30 miles north of Calcutta up the river Hooghly just off a jute mill named after no less a grandee than Queen Victoria, to a working-class settlement called Telinipara. Cleaning cups saved his life and enabled him eventually to achieve the comparative prosperity of a minor slumlord, leading in turn to convent schools for his grandchildren. That same unfathomable destiny could so easily have sent him to a sugar plantation in Fiji or the West Indies or Mauritius, the other destinations of Biharis in search of any life which included food.

If he had landed in Fiji, what would one be? A professional dissident? And in the West Indies? One could have been playing cricket. And Mauritius? One may have been renamed Akoobar, but at least one could have devoted a substantial part of one's life to having fun. This is an island which is not content with looking beautiful; it also looks happy. People smile, not because they want something out of you but because they want you to share their smile.

Mixing business with pleasure is perfectly acceptable when not actually encouraged. One's hotel is not among the pretty facades in the centre of Port Louis, the capital, but on the northern beachfront: to reach it you drive across the length of the country; if you want to go out for dinner later you might have to drive across the breadth. The Trous aux Biches must be complimented for honesty beyond the call of duty: the beach looks precisely as it does in the advertisements. Every advertisement for Paradise tends to have a topless woman stretched across the shoreline, head buried in the warm sand, the rest of the body lying in translucent waters lapping over the skin. At the Trous aux Biches this is fact. There is no surf crashing onto the shore; the loudest sound is the splash of children thrashing about in two or three feet of water. The Indian Ocean is a giant swimming pool; you can sit crosslegged or lie back on your elbows and watch the sinking sun turn the sea red as it scampers home in the evening after a full day's work. Twilight then paints the sky and the sea, as a crescent moon bridges the hour-long gap between day and night.

Morning arrives early and brings with it a light breeze which wafts the senses as gently as the soft murmur of water so clear you could drink it but for the salt. By ten or eleven the topless tourists have arrived from France or Germany, not in hordes admittedly, to soak in a sun that they will not see in their own countries till April. One is, however, constrained to mention that some of the topless middle-aged women could have found some use for a bra: there is no point, is there, if there is no point.

CIRCA ELEVEN (THAT IS the way time travels here, circuitously) the Bihari workmen have come to the patch of sand in front of the room to repair something or the other. Clearly the task requires a great deal of preliminary conversation, the pidgin Bhojpuri-French arousing volcanic emotions in a Bihari heart. No matter how much the zealous French and then the stern English might have wanted to convert the Biharis into servants of a modern economy, we have remained loyal to our incarnation as devotees of a less tense god. Some of the young men are wearing earrings: clearly, they watch television, which is a healthy sign.

After a while a supervisor drifts in, distinguished by a paunch and bearing in one hand his symbol of power, a hacksaw. But he cannot strike terror in the hearts of his fellow-Biharis. Within a few minutes they are all smiling and holding a conference on the merits of the job to be done.

Mauritius has the only Biharis who can speak French, who cannot recognise Lalu Prasad Yadav and could handily win the award for the best-dressed Biharis in the world. Some young men have turned up on the beach: tall, dark, handsome, young, fit beach boys. They spread trinkets in front of the women dotting the sand. Sales are instant among the middle-aged and an objective correspondent must report a substantial degree of friendly chatter both preceding and succeeding the official transaction. Other Bihari beach boys are stretching out like Vishnu: one toe in the netherworld, their centre touching earth and the big toe of the second leg sloping up towards heaven. Oil glistens on their dark skin and they flex their turbulent bodies with the ease of exercise-addicts.

By the afternoon the sea is so safe that parents can leave their children alone, to the mutual satisfaction of both. A five-year-old brother picks up his kid sister, throws her on his shoulders and ducks to teach her familiarity with water: one shriek from her is pure terror, the second is pure delight. Within half an hour or so the little girl is splashing about alone, and singing the first three words of '*Hot, hot, hot...*', which constitute the sum total of her knowledge of the subject. (Incidentally, does the song actually possess a few more words? This writer would like to know.)

Bihar has not been so happy since the time of Emperor Ashoka.

Later, wise men tell this writer that he should not be taken in by superficial reality: there are problems, problems, problems.... The Indians are divided: the Tamil will not empathise with the Telugu and neither will be at peace with the Bihari. The Hindu surge, they point out, has a, well, um, er, what-you-might-call-it, a saffron tinge. The Muslims, as usual, are wrapped so tightly in their search for an Islamic identity that they refuse to participate in any other reality. But disunity within and unity against the outsider is precisely what is Indian, isn't it?

THE IMPORTANT NEWS IS that Channel 2 on the Airbus 340 and Channel 3 on the Boeing 767 of Air Mauritius bring their 'special selection of good music from Mauritius and our friends and neighbours around the Indian Ocean and beyond' with a song called *Hamaar Phool* sung by Shashi. The lyrics echo Patna and Benares; the beat could only have come from Mauritius. The Biharis of Mauritius have begun to conquer the anguish of their history.

Which leaves one with a desolate question: why are the Biharis who were never sent as indentured labour, who led the nation's freedom movement against British rule, disappearing into quagmire inside India? Bihar has gone to Mauritius and transformed it; why cannot a bit of Mauritius come to Bihar? The highways of the island compare with anything in the developed world; why do the roads to Nalanda and Gaya have to be riven by potholes and surrounded by brigands? The chaos of loot has destroyed the Bihari in Bihar.

Is there a solution? In the 1860s Bihar exported Biharis. In the last decade of the twentieth century the time has come to export all the politicians of Bihar. The only problem is, which part of the world would accept such shoddy goods? Not even Mauritius.

4

1 AUGUST 1999

SOUTH BY SOUTH EAST: SOME FTS IN SOUTH AFRICA

TRAVEL CONTINUES TO BROADEN the mind and slim the wallet, which every journeyman knows. But a jet aircraft has placed some serious discord between need and necessity: the need for sleep, for instance, versus the necessity of scheduled meetings. The distance between continents is measured by the arc of the sun: the sun tends to get up long before you do or, worse, you get up long before the sun. Jet lag, unlike chill or fever from changing climates, does not even seem a respectable thing to complain about. However, since modern travel is impossible without optimism, particularly in a week when one has touched five cities in six days across two continents, I intend to count my blessings and paste them on a notice board. The notice board follows. The key symbol will be FT, for Friendly Things, as in Friendly Things that happened this week.

The FT on the first leg of the journey, from Delhi to Mumbai, is the destination. Civilisation has divested God of sole responsibility for the weather in which we function; the extremes of nature are modified in the air, which is conditioned by human hand through the alchemy of electricity. Alas, those of us condemned to live in Delhi have only a fleeting relationship with electricity. It is a relief to feel the gentle whip of rain across the face in Mumbai after the hell fire of Delhi. Never has grey been more welcome, or thunder sounded more like a chorus. The enthusiasm for monsoon ebbs just a little later that night on the South African Airways flight from Mumbai to Johannesburg as the plane moves into a band of surreal light a few minutes after takeoff: we are at about 10,000 feet and wading through clouds ablaze with unceasing lightning. Calm returns a very long minute or two later. The FT on the flight is the South African red Shiraz wine, which starts off as an acquaintance but quickly develops into a friend. I wish I could have felt as friendly towards the post-midnight snack packed in Mumbai by someone who has convinced the South Africans that this is an 'ethnic' meal.

In Johannesburg, Malcolm is our resident FT: he has been managing Vijay Mallya's 25,000-acre Mabula Game Reserve and his passion for game, adventure and conversation overlap. We hear a non-stop narrative on a lion's or a rhino's aches, pains and love life detailed with methodical fecundity. (Apparently lions have to do it every 15 minutes when the lioness is on heat and each conception may need as many as 300 to 500 couplings. Tough.) Malcolm loses his voice only once, when he is stunned into silence during dinner at a Japanese restaurant that has the Great Wall of China on display as a major icon.

The FT at the Durban Hilton the next day is the weighing machine, which indicates I am still holding up at something short of danger zone. I cannot however place the receptionist at the counter among the FTs; she smiles at my credit card rather than at me.

The FT Index peaks on Friday at the Mabula Game Reserve, a seamless sanctuary north of Johannesburg and south of the Kruger National Park. The friendliest thing at Mabula is the lion. After a substantial variety of giraffe, zebra, wildebeest, springbok, buffalo, driving around huge tunnels bored through by aardvarks, we cross a passage protected by iron gates into some 2,000 hectares kept aside as a home for a pride of lions. We locate them through a maze of radio messages in Afrikaans. Actually, the lion sees us first; we are its tourist attraction before he becomes our tourist attraction. His body is indistinguishable against the brush, but his massive head encased in a huge halo of scraggly mane is in our direct line of vision. We try to look back from our now still Land Rover as equals. His answer is to insult us. He rolls over and goes back to sleep; we are clearly too boring for any more attention. To add injury to insult, he wiggles a little, eyes still shut, waves his paws in the air and yawns. The lioness,

15 yards to his left, has more attitude. Her tail twitches as we drive towards her. Our ranger explains that she is apprehensive. This is understandable. She is guarding both her cubs and their food. They had made a substantial kill that morning – we parked next to the blood of a kudu, or antelope, a few feet from her and were on watch while two other lionesses beside her slept and two cubs watched from the back with the curiosity of children. The lazy lion could not have cared less. But the gossip about him, I am afraid, is not good. He is not very politically correct. He is an MCC (Male Chauvinist Cat). His principal ambition in life apparently is to assert his dominance over the women, which he does by exercising first rights over the food that the women have hunted. He drives the women and the children away, hitting them with his paws if necessary, until he has had his fill and he can eat up to one-twentieth of his weight. Only after that is the rest of the pride allowed to eat. I did not know that lions were role models for so many humans.

There is still a sense of wonder at the unimaginable change that has taken place in South Africa in just five years. Generations that were ready to end their lives in silent, humiliated graves have suddenly discovered the joy of an equal voice. The surprise is in the limits of excess, rather than the stories of corruption or inefficiency or ministerial indulgence that swirl through the media. The one change, however, that grates across the echoes of history is the sudden rise in crime. One explanation offered is that Nigerian gangs have driven the local thugs out, raising the levels of violent crime. Everyone has a favourite mugging story, or at least a favourite escape story. The pilots landing the aircraft into the airport at Johannesburg ask you to be careful in the city – although it does cross the mind to ask whether five years ago they were similarly telling their Black passengers to ensure that they had their 'dog passes'. Black Africans had to keep an identity tag at all times on their person and were brutally treated if they were found in Whites-only areas. A friend driving me through Durban pointed to the covered bus stand which was once used exclusively by Whites, while Blacks had to suffer the sun: even public transport was regulated to ensure that there was as little a chance of interracial communication as possible. The laws of course have now changed but the cities are still divided by the past. Except for the wealthiest zones. In a city like Durban, Indians are moving into the most expensive houses being sold by the upper class Afrikaners leaving the country.

Indians were in the middle of the apartheid sandwich, a one per cent loaf below a thin ruling class and a thick oppressed class. Their agony was not diminished by a slight difference in colour; their professional mindset, their investment in education and their urge for self-respect clashed sharply with the laws and mores of a unique, brutal system. There was nothing they could do, except wait for a miracle, delivered eventually by an authentic political saint, Nelson Mandela. Nothing has distinguished this heroic life than the manner in which Mandela has walked away from power: after five years he has simply handed over to a successor, a triumphant gesture of confidence in his nation and in his people. (Consider how we would have remembered Jawaharlal Nehru if he had actually resigned, as he wanted to, after the 1957 elections. What a waste and what a tragedy the years from 1957 to 1964, when he died heartbroken, turned out to be.)

Suddenly the Indians have found their feet, moving effortlessly into the professional echelons vacated for those who need a home elsewhere in the world. Under the old regime the best that they could hope for was to be accountants; today they can drive the economy forward. The opportunity is creating a different sort of strain as Indians become wedged above an emerging African middle class but that is a tension that should be handled with a mature balance between the give and the take. The one question that I always wanted to ask Indians and did so in their city, Durban, was why they never wanted to return to India even during apartheid. The answer I got had the velocity of truth. India was too dirty, they said. For those who have read his work, this should be called the Naipaul Syndrome.

TEDDY, WHO IS DRIVING me around in Durban, wants to know if I have ever been to Navsari; it is a fishing village in Gujarat and he comes from a family of fishermen who found their way to this port city a century or more ago. There are two FM channels playing Hindi and Tamil music in between advice to pregnant mothers. He shows me around the Soorat Hindu Society building and the mosque where a certain Haji is offering free lunch with a Milad-un-Nabi at the community hall. There is an Indian fish market, which we do not enter; and a building full of Indian shops outside which hawkers sell trinkets and local brew in foreign brandy and whisky bottles. The people look happy and are at peace with themselves. Shop names indicate the spread of Indian ownership; Teddy tells me that the Whites-only shopping streets are surrendering to the shifting laws of commerce. There are crowds and traffic jams on Warwick Street, once the dividing line between colours. He points out the street where he grew up. He has moved from there but he gets agitated by the rising violence in his neighbourhood. He is not certain where his country is headed now. So does he want the old system back? He snaps out of his anger immediately. No no no.

SUNSET IN AFRICA SIGNALS a renewal of life. We are on the top of Dick's Hill in the Mabula Game Reserve. The sun, which was sitting on a flat horizon along our drive, now wears a flushed look as it begins to sink into the curves of three waves of blue mountains in the distance. The cotton clouds have become a painter's palette, and the sky an overhead easel. The colours change as nature mixes them. The light swarms across half the sky much after the sun has disappeared. Venus appears high above the horizon, the first and only star for a long while; she will remain the brightest when the sky has become confetti. Our young barman offers us sundowners with shy courtesy, accepted with many thanks. A bonfire becomes the magnet for the small group; the fire burns up distinctions of job and status; the firewater tranquillises the nerves and loosens laughter out of our reserves. The young man at the bar, Mikhel, explains the stars to me: Mars, red and possibly furious at being in retrograde mode, is right above our heads, at a direct 90 degrees angle. The young man has never been to an astrologer but he too believes that the times will not be right when Mars is retrograde. The Southern Star brightens into a luminous pattern and he explains how sailors find their direction in the seas of the southern hemisphere: there is no Polar Bear here. The Milky Way sweeps across the sky like a ghost sleeping upon the universe. A meteor shoots its way past darkness, leaving me to wish for more hours of magic. Mikhel tells me that he enjoys his work but he wants to see the world and will work his way through the cities of his dreams: I wish the young Afrikaner luck and help if he wanders his way towards my country. Laughter gurgles a few feet away: Bob, who has Hollywood looks and an impassive mien, tells a story of an Indian politician who came to visit South Africa. The story is too funny for words, which is one of the reasons why I am not repeating it. In the circle of warmth around the bonfire, stories of the past are told and ideas about the future tossed between friends who wish the best for one another. It is a small group, but gathered from wildly different points of the human compass. Colour and caste and creed and all that couldn't divide human beings have dissolved into a wondrous rainbow pool filled by nature. This is what South Africa should be. This is what South Africa can become.

If It's Europe It Must Be a Holiday

1

9 SEPTEMBER 2001

A FOREIGNER'S DICTIONARY

MALLORCA: A GUIDE TO keywords in the English language in the unlikely event that you have to go for some work in London and need to stop over in Alcudia, Mallorca on your way back for some harder work (like staying out with friends till four in the morning at El Castita in Porto Pollento).

glum: a state of never-mind. As glum as an Englishman on the morning after the night before. Pervasive mood, consequently, at breakfast table.

breakfast: food, price always included in room rates, therefore notionally free and psychologically essential in the tourist trade. Eaten in a large room where the long face, a metaphor in English, is made physically visible particularly by those who have come on holiday with their extended families.

food (morning): anything that does not have to be cooked, as distinct from being warmed up on the assembly line. For example, eggs. A mass manufacture of standard shape, size and colour produced in farm factories. Bread: once an organic substance, now sliced into anaemic patterns sweetened in a desperate effort to improve acceptability.

dinner: cooked and therefore paid for. These days, always some part Indian in spirit if not actuality. Also known as India's Revenge on the Raj, especially when spiced to disguise quality of cooking.

Englishwoman: the best thing about an Englishman. But even the best is not sufficient to make an Englishman smile in the morning.

Compensates by smiling for two over orange juice and not necessarily in the husband's direction.

smile: that burst of radiance that envelops the face of every Spanish waiter and waitress the moment the English tourists have finished breakfast.

youth: a decibel level.

sea (Spanish): a calm body of water fringed by exotic hills out of Hollywood movies and covered by a blue sky out of Paradise. Beside a meagre strip of sand heavily populated by a succession of bodies in search of some colour other than the pale, ashen white that Nordic, Germanic and Anglo-Saxon tribes from the northern fringes of the civilised world (see Asterix) were unfortunate enough to be born with. Hordes of these northern people come south to Spain and Italy in the desperate hope that if they leave their grey, wet, blustery, gloomy homeland every six months, take off all their clothes and burn themselves in the sun they will begin to look as glamorous as those brown people who have, through history, populated the nerve centre of civilisation. Some of these worshippers of the Sun God tend to exhibit familiar symptoms of ecstasy and remove all their clothes while in that strange mood of immobile trance that affects them under the sun. The Sun God, a wanton and cruel deity, is not necessarily respectful of such devotion and is known to laugh at midday as white skin burns to lobster red instead of maturing into tender brown.

nudity: too often, an exercise in irrelevance. As has been noted before, what is the point if there is no point?

sea (English): the source and sustenance of the Spanish economy. As in: one look at the English sea and you immediately book a holiday in Spain.

rain (English): an English sea in the sky. Plus, it drips.

room service: a mysterious reality in Spanish hotels with all the characteristics of an apparition or ghost in an English castle. Everyone knows that it exists but no one has seen it.

religion: everyone has seen it, but no one knows where it is. This is official. On Wednesday 5 September 2001, Cardinal Cormac Murphy-O'Connor (real name), Archbishop of Westminster, confirmed this while assessing the state of religion in modern Britain at a gathering of a hundred select priests in Leeds. He intoned, 'Christianity as a background to people's lives and moral decisions and to the government and to the social life of Britain has almost been vanquished.' This was also evidence that syntax was in serious trouble in the Church. 'There is an indifference to Christian values and to the Church among many young people,' said Father Murphy-O'Connor, who is old enough to be a cardinal. Christianity, he explained, has been defeated by alcohol, drugs and recreational sex (as opposed to procreational sex advised by the Roman Catholic Church and no sex at all advised by the Puritans). The youth of Great Britain responded, separately and collectively, in conversation and on television, by giving the Archbishop a huge raspberry before returning to recreational sex.

holidays: the prevalent form of religion.

weather (British): the reason for modern holidays.

weather (British, archaic): the reason of the British Empire. The secret power that drove generations of Britons to farflung corners of the known and unknown (unknown to Britain, that is, but known to everyone else) world. Research at a brilliantly convivial dinner party has confirmed that if the English had better weather they would have stayed at home. Why would they want to conquer India except for the sunshine? Since there were no holiday packages available in the eighteenth and nineteenth centuries, the British had no option except to declare war, win and settle down in sunshine country. Look at Australia. They first sent prisoners and then when they received reports of sunshine, the rest followed. As the poet of the British Empire has noted, mad dogs and Englishmen go out in the midday sun. Why did the English never want to conquer France or Germany or, God forbid, Russia? Who would want to rule nations with the same, or worse, weather? Makes no sense. The English are not Germans. Or not nearly enough. Money is not as important as sunshine.

money: something that you change at the counter of the first available official crook, often gurgling thanks. Waiting for a better rate is so stupid that I am appalled I even thought of it.

taxi-driver: someone who knows what to do with your money. If the taxi-driver is sour, you get milked. If he is friendly, you get soaked.

peseta: a low currency in a high economy. Higher than the lira but lower than the rupee. It sounds good to learn that there are twice as many pesetas to the dollar than rupees, but don't overdo the celebrations.

conversation: a discussion on cricket.

cricket: a rich man's game without money. Therefore, open to corruption. Once an Englishman's honour, now a vehicle for upwardly mobile Asians. Also, an expression of Australian nationalism, with special emphasis on grinding to dust descendants of those who ruled a well-advertised empire. In Britain, a game undergoing radical emotional surgery while in the process of being handed over to Asian immigrants. By 2007 there is likely to be, by law, only one token white in the English cricket team. The best of white talent is shifting to football.

football: a poor man's game with money. Becoming, consequently, more respectable by the day. Once a definition of working class grit, now a vehicle for upwardly mobile Africans and South Americans. By 2007 even football could change colour. At the moment, however, it is on a pinnacle, with England having scored their greatest victory since the Second World War. Coincidentally, both these victories were against Germany. In 1945 also Germany lost 5-1 to Churchill.

Donald Trelford: reason for being in Mallorca on the way home from a hard stint in London. A very old and handsome friend with a very young and beautiful wife. In constant difficulties because of a large heart. Born a Christian but should have been a Muslim. He could then have lived with all his wives. With the youngest as the favourite, of course.

2

3 FEBRUARY 2002

PRINCE AU PORT: A PORTUGAL DIARY

LISBOA: PORTUGAL IS FATIMAH, the holy mother of Jesus who is worshipped and adored; Fada, their traditional music, which is still giving strong competition to pop and rock; and Football, which they adore but do not worship. I am sure there is another F on the list of recreations, but being Catholic they don't mention it. Where else but on the Iberian Peninsula would a footballer be punished for atheism? In the last week of January 2002 Oscar Tellez, who plays as a defender for the club Deportivo Alaves, was fined 750 euros because he did not go to church. To give you the whole story: a funeral mass was being held for the obviously departed honorary president of the club, Jose Luis Companon, which the team was ordered to attend. Oscar went up to the door of the church, and stayed there. He explained: 'I didn't enter the church because I don't like churches, and I don't believe in what goes on inside them.' Fair enough. Or not. The club did not take kindly to this explanation and decided to make Oscar an example before the club and community. 'I don't know why they have to force a player to enter a church,' argued Oscar. 'What would happen if the club signed up a player who observes Ramadan or doesn't eat meat? Would he be forced to eat or would he be punished too?' No point in wondering about all that, Oscar. It is highly unlikely that Deportivo Alaves is going to sign practising Muslims or Hindu vegetarians from Churchill Brothers in their crusade for the conquest of the first division league title.

THE TOURIST LITERATURE NEVER quite admits it, but Portugal did not exist before the Muslims. The peninsula was populated by the Celtic and Gothic tribes (made famous in the contemporary world by Asterix and Obelix) before and during the Roman occupation. In 711 the Muslims arrived with a small army of about 12,000 soldiers and retained their hold until the fall of the great Nasirids of Granada in 1499. Muslims ruled what is now Portugal for 400 years until Afonso Henriques took the marvellous fort on the highest hill of the city of Lisboa in 1148 and created an independent kingdom. For 350 years after that Muslims and Jews continued to live in Portugal as citizens rather than rulers until the spirit of the Spanish Inquisition seized Manuel in the last decade of the fifteenth century. He ordered every Muslim and Jew to either convert within ten months of his orders, or leave the country. This might have been a comparatively generous option but for a rider. Children below fifteen would be forcibly converted in any case, so parents were given a choice between their children and their faith. The Muslims who chose to leave went across the Atlantic to Morocco, carrying the keys of their homes in the hope that one day they would be allowed to return. Where did the Jews go? To the Ottoman Empire, where the sultans of Turkey gave them protection and a place in their empire for which they were ever grateful. This is one of the reasons why relations between Turkey and Israel have always remained better than between Israel and any other Muslim country. When, during the turn of the fourteenth into the fifteenth century the aggressive Spanish rulers of Castile tried to absorb Portugal into Spain, King John successfully defended the integrity of Portugal and became a hero to his people. In 1455 Pope Nicholas V in a famous Bull gave Portugal the mission to take the holy war to Africa and India; later, to prevent a clash of local Iberian civilisations, Rome divided the world between Portugal and Spain. The former got the east and the latter the west of what was called the Pope's Line. It is instructive to note that Portugal reached India in 1499 and established a kingdom in Goa sixteen years before Babur reached Delhi. Portugal was also the last to leave, fourteen years after the British. Stubborn.

IF PORTUGAL CONTINUES TO live in Goan life, then Goa also continues to live in the Portuguese language. Let me place a note of warning: the following may be injurious to the health of those who believe otherwise. I am repeating only what I heard from certain sources.

The word for mother is *mae* and comes from the Indian *mai*. We have given jungle to English as well; in Portugal it has become *janela*. *Cha* for tea is not very surprising, but they use *fita* for laces, *sono* for sleep (our *sona*), *nau* for boat, *almira* for, well, almirah which derives from *almari* and *mesa* for table – from our very own *mez*. *Pao* is *pao*; no explanations required, surely, for that. Even a verb like *dena* has become *da/dou,* while the human feet are *perna,* a variation of *payr*. Some words we assume to be Portuguese or at least European come from our very own motherland: *reina* from *rani* for queen, *padre* from *padri* and *chama* from *shama* or flame. However, I am just a shade doubtful whether *vejo* is a variation of the Punjabi *vekhyo* but doubtless there is a jury out there among readers who will correct me if I have been less than just to Punjabi international influence. I am indebted for this list to the bright, young and idealistic Indian Foreign Service officer in our embassy, Randhir Jaiswal, which gives me another opportunity to blame the government for any of my mistakes. The most poignant word that has travelled so many thousands of miles is *duvida,* the Portuguese word for our Hindi *duvidha*. No one can come to India, live for five and a half centuries and return home without a touch of *duvidha*.

If you want to see Goa perched on top of a mountain, go to Obidos. The main church of this fortified village, with a sweeping view of the Atlantic from its height, at the northern end of the Rue Direita, was a mosque for 400 years and a tribal temple of the Visigoths before it became a mosque. So it goes. The battlements were built by the Moors and provide some idea of why these fortresses were so impregnable. A group of schoolgirls, crowned like princesses, were assembled outside the church when we ambled past, the starting point of their lesson in visual history. Amble is the correct word; hurry would be unfair to the serene spirit of Obidos. The walls of the small houses are white, the roofs are tiled and flowers tumble out of curved verandah grilles. A cocker spaniel guards an empty shop, sitting perfectly still. It would be impolite to bark. There is a domestic air about the commerce. Shops may or may not have shopkeepers, until you step in when someone next door interrupts a chat to check if you are a paying customer or a window shopper. There are two kinds of shops: one for tourists who believe that they must take home things that they will not use and cannot gift away, it's so embarrassing. The second are the shops whose products you are unlikely to give away even if you buy them as gifts: the superb wine and the outstanding port. They drink port through the day and who can blame them? Add the splendid fresh fish that they pick up from the Atlantic, throw in the sunshine that is unaffected by winter (a jacket is good enough in January), mix all this with the smile that they happily offer and you have the magic recipe for tourists. Goa has contributed to the menu with a European version of prawn masala. Along with this order at the restaurant of the Hotel da Torre, which I could hardly resist, turned up papad. Will there come a day when we shall do unto the Portuguese what we have done with the British? They took over the economy; we have taken over their food. I call this justice of history.

PORTUGAL, THEY SAY, COMES from port, the dark sweet wine. It could easily come from the port on the confluence of the Tejo, a river of African and Asiatic dimensions, and the Atlantic. Lisbon grew on this corner. The Tejo sparkles and laps while the Atlantic surges and roars; you would not believe that water could be so different in such proximity. The Portuguese commemorate the point from which Vasco da Gama left with three small ships for India, after a night spent in prayer at the chapel of Henry the Navigator (still simple and small). The monument to their first great admiral-captain and his heirs is marked with the great cross of the Crusades. One nation's golden age is another nation's misery: the great voyages that began here ended in horror stories along the western coast of India. Malabar was the only kingdom that resisted the Portuguese for years, through defeat and the occasional victory; Cochin betrayed Malabar and gave the Portuguese a foothold that they converted into command of the oceans from their Indian empire in Goa. The historian K.M. Pannikkar, in a telling line, writes that the only thing that the Portuguese taught India was new methods of killing and some of those means are in fact too gruesome to repeat. But that Portugal is long gone. Portugal's interest in the East is now visible in academics rather than gunboat diplomacy. The Instituto do Oriente of the Universidade Tecnica de Lisboa has an impressive new building, the river Tejo glistening through one window and woods climbing hills through the other. It is run by Professor Narana Coissoro, whose blue eyes twinkle and whose laugh booms through dinner and seminar alike. He is a Hindu who left Goa to study law in Portugal fifty years ago and is now one of the senior leaders of the government in addition to his responsibilities in the university: he still has a home and relatives in Goa. That laugh disguises a shrewd understanding of emerging Europe and a rising Asia; his role is to build the links that will nourish both. We may be entering a post-post-colonial world. Professor Narana Coissoro is also evidence that you may take Goa away from Portugal, but you cannot take Portugal away from Goa.

3

27 OCTOBER 2002

A PARIS DIARY

When you take a taxi in Paris you expect to be taken for a ride. The good news is that even a ride in Paris is enchanting. In the parks along the avenues the handsome, adult trees have turned to rust before the fall. In the stylised square garden of Louis XIII at Marais the trees are still a light bright green but there is a feel of a last flutter in the air The gardener out here is either a mathematician or a barber. The trees have been haircut into identical oblongs. In another place, another city, this affectation might have seemed gauche. Paris carries it off with panache. Louis XIII clearly took a singular decision and the citizens of this district, Marais, left their inheritance alone – it would have been gauche to interfere. The centuries-old bakeries of this *arrondisement* have become shoeshops now but are still called bakeries. Everything changes and nothing changes. The Eiffel Tower wears electricity over its steel and a lighthouse beam rotates at the top, searching for nothing more significant than attention. You can still crunch the leaves on the banks of the Seine, but the famous lovers are not around any longer to steal kisses. That stands to reason. There is nothing to steal these days, for no one has anything to hide in this age of Just Do It. Lovers do not need the silence of the Seine; they are all in their drawing rooms, searching for inspiration from television during a pause. The fact of the matter is that sex has become a matter of fact. Even in Paris.

YOU AND I SHRUG. A Parisian does not shrug. A Parisian does a tap dance with his shoulders. There is nothing indifferent or diffident about a shrug in Paris. It is full of pathos and fit for opera. The reason may be trivial, or not. The reaction is never less than momentous. When a lady in a car a good foot lower than our taxi loses the balance of her nerves in the middle of a well-structured traffic jam on the Rue Bonaparte and begins to scream, our driver responds with a Parisian shrug, some silence and then well-meaning advice on how she should spend her time home with her children before he slips through a glimmer between the cars. I can report that the authorities are trying to do something about these famous traffic jams. The Rue Rivoli, for instance, now has a separate lane for taxis and buses, although every owner of a car has not been informed of this change. The Parisian traffic settles in the mind before it congeals on the street. The Frenchman will never surrender his fundamental rights, having won them at such substantial cost 200 years ago. The primary right of the motorist is to press the accelerator with as much force as he presses the brake, in quick succession. He also has the right to gesticulate his attitude towards life with both hands while driving.

TWO CENTURIES AFTER THE first, a second French Revolution is taking place. The French are speaking English. Arguably, this achievement is on par with beheading the Bourbons, dealing with Danton, surviving the hope and despair of Napoleon and coming to terms with Waterloo. In 1815 the French accepted the victory of the English on the battlefield; they are learning to accept the victory of English in the classroom, the café and even the coiffure. Waiters now actually bring food when you ask for beef, instead of *boeuf*, throwing in an indulgent smile for free. This is a stunning philosophical and psychological somersault. It would, however, be incorrect to say that all the old fire has died out. There are still twentieth century cabdrivers who, when it is midnight and wet, curl their upper lip at the sound of English and insist, with all the familiar ardour and zeal, that they are going in exactly the opposite direction to which you desire to travel. There is a glint in their eye as they leave you stranded and miserable on the Champs D'Elysee, the warmth of an excellent meal and fine company oozing out of your pores with each icicle of rain. But these are yesterday's warriors, content with minor triumphs in meaningless skirmishes. The war is lost. English is taught in every school.

The French are, though, trying to salvage a last laugh from this horrendous defeat. An advertisement inside a train on the fast Metro between St Germain and Gare du Nord shows a young man leaping into the air because he has successfully mastered 'Wall Street English'. I had heard of cockney English, pidgin English, Indian English, Oxbridge English and BBC English. What was Wall Street English? It was a triumph of positioning. The French have bypassed the channel and moved directly across the Atlantic to Wall Street American. English has been shown its place, as it were.

THE HEADQUARTERS OF THE police and the headquarters of religion are literally next door to each other in Paris. Symbolic? Where should the wages of sin be paid? In prison or the confession box? Which is more necessary for the common good? The plain cell of the prefecture or the magnificent cathedral of Notre Dame?

One of the real dangers of this city is that even the mundane can tempt you towards philosophy. That is the power of beauty. Of all the sights of Paris nothing is grander that the Notre Dame, particularly now that the darkness of centuries has been scrubbed from its walls. The soul can search for sublimity here.

Luckily the police headquarters reminds me of *The Pink Panther*. I half expect Peter Sellers to come bumbling out, closely pursued by a tumbling Herbert Lom, both tripping into the Seine. Does my fancy exaggerate when I notice a veritable Inspector Clouseau on the street? The police officer has an expression that says that there is no point in trusting him too much. Tales of petty crime abound. I suppose they would in any city with so many tourists. Indians, of course, have the best stories. One Indian is spreading word that all he did was look up at the flight timings at Charles de Gaulle airport to find that his suitcases had vanished from under his nose. He must have taken his time to read that screen. Or maybe he was confused to find French written in the English script. When he complained to the police they apparently told him that he was the 24th person to make a similar complaint within the hour. I just hope the other 23 were not Indians from the same flight.

THE TRUE BEAUTY OF Paris is not in the tourist brochures or the sales pitch of cathedrals, however wondrous they may be. It lies in the love with which an anonymous architect has shaped the unknown cornice. Every corner of this city is a small dream; every district a collective inspiration preserved with passion. In the Second World War the French surrendered to the Germans rather than let Paris be destroyed by the Luftwaffe and artillery of Adolf Hitler. Six decades later the French have recovered the pride they lost in 1940. But if they had lost Paris as well in 1940 there would have been nothing to recover from the rubble.

It was a good bargain.

THE BEST CONTEMPORARY BARGAIN in the city could be a bar. Buddha Bar, just off the city's most fashionable shopping area behind the Torcadero and Place l'Concorde, is setting the style in evening environment, decor and music. They might want to improve their food though. Guess which song they are fusing their local genius to right now? Indipop. Things that go into the night with an Indian warble and Hindi words like *Paon mein ghungroo lagte hain...*

India has arrived, via Hollywood.

4

1 JUNE 2003
CHECKPOINT BERLIN

IT WAS AN AWESOME display of German efficiency. I have no idea how long they took to roll out the red carpet for Prime Minister Atal Behari Vajpayee at the Berlin-Tegel airport, but I am eyewitness to the reverse process. He had barely stepped off the hallowed wool when, out of some mysterious space in the air, three spirits materialised. Incidentally, or coincidentally, they were clad in brilliant red sweaters and jogging trousers. They took position at the top of the carpet. An order crackled in the thin rain, like a gunshot at the start of a race. On the further edge a woman sprinted, tearing the wide tape that secured the red carpet to the black tarmac. The other two, man and woman, caught the carpet on the roll as it were, as it was being released from the tape, and whirled it up at running pace till it vanished into a thick circle.

VIPs come and go. The tarmac stays black for ever.

BERLIN BEGINS AT THE gate of the airport. There is no pause for a highway. You hit a traffic jam on the first turn. Perhaps Berliners felt safer within walking distance of their lifeline to the West when the Cold War froze their lives. This was the frontier city of this war, isolated and disputed in the middle of East Germany. It was the prize that the Soviet Union and the West nearly blew up the world for. There was nothing left to blow up in Berlin itself, because American and British bombers had already done that in the last year of the Second World War. Some stark symbols have been preserved from a century of blood-river politics. In front of our hotel, at the top of Kurfuerstendamm, the street that has been host to both cabaret and spies, stands a cathedral without a spire, its jagged top cutting the air, its sculptured walls gaping with bombed craters. This is what the cathedral looked like when Berlin fell to the Allies in 1945, and this is what they have left it as: a memory of pain sublimated by faith. This cathedral without a cause has only one thing that works, golden clocks that tell the time, accurately and inexorably.

A THIN WALL SOUNDS like an oxymoron. The Berlin Wall was the first modern wall. It was thin and it was low. The age of battering rams and sieges was over. The wall was a paradox. It was not designed to keep the invader out. It was erected to imprison its own citizens, to prevent their escape to a better life.

To partition a country is a tragedy. To divide a city is obscene. The Communists needed thin concrete, cutting wire, searching lights and cocked guns to protect their paradise. They separated neighbours with fear. Berlin held its breath and waited thirty years before an edifice cracked in Russia and emotions were released with volcanic fury in Germany. Berliners brought the wall down, slab by joyous slab. Like the cathedral they have left parts of it standing to nourish memory with architecture that has become the art of shards.

IF A WALL CAN ever be said to have a heart, then Checkpoint Charlie was the heart of the Berlin Wall. This was the very American name of the gate in the US sector through which official – and, more deliciously, unofficial – traffic passed. Desolate sandbags and a fluttering Stars and Stripes mark the crossroads of superpower games played with spies, economists, armies and nuclear missiles. Spies, fortunately, generated far more literature than the rest put together. Berlin was the theatre of all the great spy stories.

Windblown scraps of paper still litter the approach to Checkpoint Charlie. You walk across what was once deathly no-man's-land towards occasional remnants of the wall. An ornate, heavy and archaic building looms up. This used to be Goebbels' office. In front, adjacent to a park, is a narrow quarry of concrete boxes some six feet below ground level. This is one of the concentration camps in which the fascist Nazis sent Jews, gypsies and other untouchables to slave or die. The gas pipes that administered the final solution have also been preserved. Lest we forget.

It is a bleak square mile, appropriately sparse, stark and unrelieved by either the green of the earth or the sunshine in the sky. Even the museum at Checkpoint Charlie is sombre, despite being full of victory tags collected by the winning side in the Cold War. The only smile on the windowscape of the museum is toothless and familiar. A picture of Mahatma Gandhi dominates the entrance. Gandhi is the messenger and the message amid the historical debris of so much war. Non-violence.

THE FIRST BIT OF graffiti that I saw as we drove out of the airport into the traffic jam said, simply: 'F**k War!' Chancellor Gerhard Schroeder won re-election last year, 2002, because he did precisely that. My little quarrel with the suggestion is actually a self-question. Why do newspapers continue to place two blanks in that four-letter word when every English-speaker whose age is in double digits has heard the word in the movies and knows what it means? Only those whose age is in three digits don't know what it means anymore.

To recreate the past is stupid, said a bureaucrat who was building the future. Devastated by the warm war and distorted by the cold one, Berlin became an invitation to an idea when it was restored as the capital of reunified Germany. The new Germany sought to soften its image of a harsh, war-hungry past through a marvellous resurrection of nature. Berlin, like other German cities, is alive with greenery, trees and parks and, occasionally, even dense foliage. A river like Isar in Munich, actually just an adult canal, sometimes seems to be speeding through a jungle. There is public art everywhere, on streets and open spaces, impressively comforting. The new government buildings in Berlin are light, sunny and minimalist, in deliberate contrast to the Gothic, columned, high and dense structures of an aggressive past. The future is going to be fashioned out of a minimalist present. The past is over. One of Hitler's offices, I am informed by a friend who is an exile from Dhaka, has now become an Indian restaurant owned by a Bangladeshi. If Hitler had been accorded a grave, he would be churning in it.

MUNICH, CAPITAL OF BAVARIA in the south of Germany, was the political capital of the Nazi movement. It was in Bavaria that Hitler first tried to seize power, in 1923, but was stopped. Hitler's first mass demonstrations took place here, in a city whose name means 'a monk's place'. Munich was given its first trading and currency rights by Emperor Friedrich Barbarossa, who took the most powerful Crusader army ever assembled towards Jerusalem. He might have changed that wayward course of history if he had not drowned in a stream on his way to Damascus. Hitler named his invasion of the Soviet Union, which changed the course of his history, Operation Barbarossa. Would that Hitler had drowned on the way!

WE REACHED THE FREE State of Bavaria (which lost its independence only in 1933) on 29 May, a regional holiday to celebrate the ascension of the Virgin Mary to heaven. This province on the border of Italy is Catholic country and takes religion seriously. The ruling party is known as the Christian Social Union and wins office with ease. Truth to tell, the whole of Germany takes religion more seriously than the rest of Europe. Every citizen has to indicate on his tax form whether he is a believer or not. Every Christian believer has to pay a 'church tax' of two and a half per cent over and above the 40 per cent tax payable by high income groups. This seems a Christian variation of the Islamic *zakat*, by which two and a half per cent of your wealth must be donated to charity every year. The Church Tax pays the salaries of priests and renovates church buildings of both Catholic and Protestant alike. In return, the church provides society not only with food for divine thought, but also crèches for babies. This is an important service in a society where all women work and state schools care for the child after Class I.

Martin Luther was a German, but after more than half a millennium the Protestant zeal seems to have diminished. There is a growing desire to return to a single, perhaps non-denominational, Church. The Catholics have, however, neither forgotten nor forgiven. The Vatican recently reminded its followers that they could not take communion from any priest except that of the Catholic Church.

UNNECESSARY FACT OF THE Week: The much-married Chancellor Gerhard Schroeder does not dye his hair. Why is this news? Because he almost lost the election after a magazine alleged that he secretly dyed his hair. Schroeder sued and the controversy dyed a natural death. I can confirm that when we saw the Chancellor for about half an hour in Berlin, the grey had begun to show.

5

19 OCTOBER 2003

AUSCHWITZ: HORROR, FROZEN

CRACOW, POLAND: SERENITY IS sitting in the sky at 33,000 feet on A clear afternoon watching the earth pass by. The land between Britain and Poland has soaked more human blood than any other comparable stretch. The great wonder of our age is surely the peace that Europe has woven from the torn shreds of a mutilated history: even the Cold War is over. Britain and Poland will form the western and eastern boundaries of the European Union after May 2004, when Poland along with nine other countries is admitted. The British Airways plane basks in the warmth of an autumn sun that encourages a sense of good cheer. The air hostess, who has been laughing insistently and on occasion infectiously, insists that the wine on my tray is wrong and switches it to the Pic Saint-Loup Reserve, a '*Produit of France*'. It is an excellent decision. The red wine has been named after a hermit who apparently lived on the summit of a mountain that bears his name, situated between the Mediterranean and Montpellier. I don't know how close the hermit came to God from that summit, but he certainly did a lively line in reds. Clouds appeared after we crossed the English Channel: light, fluffy, square pieces of cotton that formed rows of extraordinary straight lines like the parade of a benevolent, slightly slipshod army. The sky became a bit more dense as we neared our destination, Cracow, the old capital of Poland and on the UNESCO list of the world's 12 most remarkable architectural complexes. The first mention of the city in a document has been dated to 965, when a Jewish merchant from Muslim Spain, Ibrahim ibn Yaqub, left a record of his visit. A sharp breeze welcomed me outside the modest airport, but the real weather was measured by the warmth of friends waiting for me. There are days when life seems too short. This was one of them.

A TRUMPET BLAST FROM A tower at the corner of Market Square begins powerfully and ends abruptly. They still commemorate the moment when a dutiful watchman warned the city in the thirteenth century that the Tartars were invading Cracow. The abrupt end came when a Tartar arrow slit the watchman's throat. The story has a happy ending, which presumably is why they remember it. The citizens rallied and repelled the Tartars on that occasion but of course the Tartar invasion of Poland has many more chapters. There are still some 10,000 Muslim Tartars in Poland.

The square is dominated by the Church of the Virgin Mary, unprepossessing outside but resplendent inside. This Sunday they are celebrating the 25th anniversary of the papacy of Karol Wojtyla, their most famous priest and now Pope John Paul II. Faith may have disappeared from the rest of Europe, but Poland remains a deeply religious country. Even Stalin did not dare eliminate the Church from Polish lives. He remarked that putting Poles under Communist atheism would be like placing a saddle around a cow. The splendour of the Church of the Virgin Mary was doubly dazzling in the light of a live service. Every generation contributed its genius to a social monument and museum of faith. The two imposing towers at the entrance begin symmetrically but end differently; one is higher. The story goes that they were built by two brothers, competing for the glory of God. When the elder completed the north tower, he killed his younger sibling to prevent the south tower from rising beyond his structure. The knife he used is preserved in the church.

Poles take their faith seriously, but never so seriously as to deny themselves a joke. A rabbi was invited by a cardinal to see the glories of his church. Each wall, each corner, each square inch of space was packed with treasures: a feast of jewellery, paintings, tapestry, chandeliers and rising altars in gold. The rabbi looked around and asked the cardinal: 'Where is the space for God in this church?'

THE ONLY SKYSCRAPERS IN Cracow are church steeples, which is a good thing. Plaster peels off the walls of innumerable homes, which is not. The city is an extraordinary mix of castles, cathedrals, and compounds that look like a backdrop from a fifties' neo-realist Italian movie. All this will change in five years, when the economic and social laws of the European Union take over the city. This has been Poland's consuming mission ever since its liberation from the Soviet empire at the turn of the nineties and it will realise its dream on 1 May 2004. Not every Pole was keen to join the Union, with its *laissez faire* attitudes. One of the slogans of the nay-sayers was: 'Vote for the European Union! It will become much easier for your son to find a husband!'

But the need to join NATO and then EU was understandable; Poland wanted iron-clad guarantees for its independence from Moscow. Curiously, after having achieved this, Poland now wants guarantees of independence from the European Union. Well, maybe not that curiously. Germany and France have partitioned Poland as eagerly as Moscow has swallowed it. The new mantra, therefore, is the United States of America. This craving for a special relationship has persuaded the Polish government, against the will of the majority of its own people, to send 2,000 soldiers to guard Iraq on behalf of Washington. Ease overlaps with unease in this decision. Having been a victim of occupation, Poland erases the word from public discourse; its troops are a 'stabilisation' force. There is great eagerness on the part of officials to underline the difference and suggest that their contingent is under local command for all practical purposes. This is why Polish soldiers did not intervene in a firefight of the kind on Friday, 17 October, that left three American soldiers dead. On the television screen a Polish officer in Iraq says that he has nothing to say to the media. At least in this respect, they are different from the Americans. In Warsaw, officials stress that a large number of NGOs have gone with the soldiers and that they are busy opening schools for Iraqi children. This is yet another baffling aspect of the American intervention. The Iraqis never had any shortage of schools under the Baathists or ever since the second Abbasid emperor established Baghdad more than 1,300 years ago. Every occupation needs to justify its presence by promising 'civilisation'. It is undeniable, however, that the Poles are more sensitive to local sentiment than their superpower ally. There have been no casualties so far in their contingent. But then again, they have been posted in the Shia regions of the east and the south and the real war may not have even begun there.

CRACOW UNIVERSITY WAS BUILT IN THE FOURTEENTH CENTURY, AND THANK God that they have not tried to improve it. The curse of modernisation was one of the principal socialist temptations and Cracow side-stepped it. All that it needed was heated rooms and that is a welcome change. Professors no longer have to be celibate or sit silently in square cells either reading or hearing the Bible as their principal means of education and entertainment. I am in Poland for a series of lectures and everywhere the faculty is open, discursive and enlivened by the necessary touch of the eccentric professor. Learning is a serious business, but not a grim one. The students are attentive, thoughtful and involved. I was surprised at the turnouts for the lectures, since the subject – Islam and the West – was not especially glamorous. True, the presence of their soldiers in Iraq must have played its part in provoking interest but their eyes were genuinely in search of an alternative view. They responded positively when I pointed out the first fallacy: that Islam was a faith while the West was a geography, and then suggested that this is where the thesis of civilisations might have misled them. One very real problem is that the dialogue has got trapped in words that mean totally different things in different environments. The word 'fundamentalist', for instance. A believer is defined by the fact that he believes in the fundamentals of his faith, so fundamentalism is not an accusation but a compliment. Is the Pope a fundamentalist, then, for being the guardian of the faith? A lecture never hopes to answer all questions, but if it can open the door to some questions about previously held convictions, then the effort is worthwhile.

THE WEEK HAD AGED, and the season changed. The sky had absorbed the grey ink of oncoming winter and a cold wind searched the tolerance levels of the body. A group of children laughed as they raced out of the stark, sprawling complex of prison camps, a steaming cup of coffee in their hands to challenge the cold. Children have their own ways of dealing with shock. They are less sentimental about evil than we think. They were schoolchildren from Israel and this visit to Poland was part of their transition, a defining moment in their individual and collective history; and a reminder that they were fortunate not to have lived in the times of their grandparents. We were at the Nazi concentration camps in Auschwitz.

Knowledge can never prepare you for reality. I must have read thousands of words about these camps. All of them simply evaporated in the face of what I saw. What I saw was only shards of preserved evil; the weight of the full truth leaves you crushed and helpless. The Jews were the prime target of the racist Nazis but not the only one. The poet has not been found who can describe such barbarism. Instead of words an image appeared in my mind from some distant closet of memory, a photograph of the first encounter between a group of prisoners and the first soldiers to reach Auschwitz as the Nazis fell back on the eastern front. There was absolute incredulity on the face of the liberator. There was absolute immobility on the face of the prisoner, a complete indifference to the freedom they had dared not contemplate a minute before and could not yet comprehend as real. Those prisoners had died too often in the concentration camps for them to believe anymore in life. There were times that afternoon, as I walked through the gas chambers and halls of photographs of gypsy children and mute hills of shoes and suitcases which the condemned had brought, when I felt violently ill. But you cannot even throw up when there is only emptiness inside. Anger filled the vacuum. Nothing made me angrier than the sheer banality of Nazi evil. The sign that welcomed prisoners to Auschwitz said: 'Work makes you free'. It was a joke upon the slaves, most of whom would prefer death before long. The smirk on the faces of Nazis sitting at committee meetings to count the numbers they had killed was beyond guilt. They were in a zone outside humanity and outside morality. But you could sense an undeclared sense of guilt among those who had heard the screams of people being picked up from the city ghettos and turned away to protect themselves with silence. It is always thus when demons embark on genocide.

What were the children saying as they skipped or raced back to their school bus, protecting themselves from their own feelings by a burst of energy? That life goes on? Sometimes it seems that only death goes on, whether in a Palestinian camp or a restaurant in Haifa. There are days when life seems too long.

6

27 JUNE 2004
MARBLE MAGIC

FLORENCE: THE DEFINING DIFFERENCE between the Englishman and the Italian is the gesture. An Italian speaks on the telephone with both hands, neither of which may actually hold the instrument. The phone is cradled between chin and shoulder, leaving the hand free to gesticulate while the fingers create intricate patterns to reinforce meaning to someone miles away, at the other end of the phone and therefore completely unable to see this hand-dance. The real purpose of this exercise in stress and delicacy, in other words, is to express for the sake of expression, rather than for the sake of communication. Thus every telephone conversation becomes an art form, a dance of hands and fingers to the rhythm and nuance of speech.

The Englishman from the rigid, Teutonic north does not know the potential creativity of hands. The Englishman not only has a stiff upper lip but also a stiff lower hand. John Cleese in *Fawlty Towers* may exaggerate but his excess is firmly rooted in fact: the Englishman prefers to walk or talk with his fingers pointed firmly south. The Italian of the liquid, Latino south is more like an Indian. A 'where', a 'must', a 'there', a 'what' or any of a wide range of exclamations is incomplete without the finger dance. The only time Italians throw their arms down is when they are flabbergasted. The only time an Englishman throws his arms up is when he is flabbergasted.

Is this subconscious? One must address this question in these Freudian (or perhaps just slightly post-Freudian) times. Does the

Englishman associate raising his hands with surrender, and therefore considers it beneath his dignity? Could be. These tough colonial types hate surrender and will do anything to prolong the agony of conflict rather than obey the dictates of common sense. Italians, on the other hand, so to speak, have surrendered to the pleasures of good life for countless generations. Duty doesn't call around here anymore. They did their best fighting about 2,000 years ago and now sell that memory to tourists while they concentrate on the joys of living off an extraordinarily beautiful land. Perhaps that is why Winston Churchill growled, when informed that Italy had joined Germany and the Axis Powers in the Second World War, that it was only fair: after all, Italy had been on Britain's side in the First World War. They should become someone else's handicap this time around.

WHEN WAS FLORENCE BORN? The facts are arid. It was an Etruscan village like thousands of others whose names we do not remember. Julius Caesar created Florentia (meaning flowering) in BC 59 for the best of reasons, because it was the most convenient crossing point on the river Arno for his armies. Before Caesar, the village was a mere truth; he reshaped it into reality.

The difference is magnificent. The power of Italian genius lies in its ability to lift truth to a higher dimension by a powerful vision. And so, when Florentines sneered that Michelangelo's statue of the dissolute Giuliano was too heroic to be a likeness of the wastrel son of Lorenzo the Magnificent, Michelangelo answered: 'In a thousand years no one will know how they looked!' Or, they will look as I have made them look, because my art will last a thousand years, while their bodies and their reputations will be consumed by time. Time surrenders only to art and fable.

SUCH WAS THE MYTH of the Roman Empire that it continued to be called Roman long after Rome had nothing to do with it. The term 'Roman' added legitimacy to emperors of the east and west of Europe who were Turko-Greeks, French or Germans. Florence flourished under the pagan Romans and when the Eastern Roman Empire under Constantine made Christianity legal constructed a church on the spot where the glorious cathedral now stands, overpowering an opulent city with its scale and splendour. When power shifted west, Florence was ruled for three centuries by Charlemagne's Franks. In 1100 it won independence from the Germans who had taken possession and with this began its age of glory as a city state, before bowing to Napoleon and then the Hapsburgs. In 1848 Italy began to cohere as a nation under Victor Emmanuel. Florence joined the new kingdom in 1860. Rome became the capital of modern Italy in 1870; Florence remains the capital of European art.

ANY CITY THAT CAN claim Giotto the architect, Donatello the sculptor, Benvenuto Cellini the jeweller, Dante ('I am the father of the Italian language') and Petrarch the poets, Boccaccio the storyteller, Amerigo Vespucci (now you know where America comes from) the discoverer, Galileo the scientist, and Raphael, Leonardo da Vinci and Michelangelo the artists as its children, must have superlative genes. The statues of the city's best and brightest adorn the courtyard of the Uffizi gallery, home to Europe's greatest artistic treasures. The most remarkable of the statues are those of Dante Alighieri and Niccolo Machiavelli.

Dante seems a contradiction. Could anyone so austere and purse-lipped really be in love with anyone but himself? And so Beatrice, his love and guide, must surely be an artistic conceit necessary for his journey through faith and prejudice across Paradise, Purgatory and Inferno.

Did Machiavelli really look that Machiavellian? The Florentines certainly think so. His eyes glitter in stone. They slant to the right as if a direct gaze would be too honest. A smile of high intelligence and low craft plays upon his lips. His head is bent forward, his shoulders seem to participate in a ploy, tilting to hide a stratagem. Those familiar with *The Prince* know that it is more realpolitik than ruthless but the statue is a fine image of cunning. I did not find the cunning despicable. It was craft in service of power, not the craft of a moneylender who steals from the poor. And yet it made me shudder. For this was an image of power unhinged, of power without morality, or power unredeemed by any idea of service. The dharma of such power was only more power.

I have not seen a statue of Chanakya. My image of him comes from a reading of *Arthashashtra*, a cool treatise rather than a cold one, untrammelled by sentiment but as heavily anchored to the good of the state as to the good of the monarch. I can see why Jawaharlal Nehru once flirted with the idea of becoming a Chanakya, even as he laughed at himself for such fantasising. He had no time for Machiavelli.

A story illustrates the difference. Chanakya, after winning a kingdom for his prince, Chandragupta Maurya, sought permission to retire and return to Takshila. Chandragupta was aghast, for this was the time to reap the rewards of victory and rule. But for Chanakya, this was enough. He had a last word of advice to the new monarch. He should make the defeated general a commander of his armies. This, said Chanakya, is the best guarantee of future peace. The lesson applies in today's politics as well. The first thing to do in victory is to woo the next enemy, not make an enemy of a potential ally.

Machiavelli went to prison and died powerless because he was too much in love with power. Chanakya died in peace because he knew the limits and limitations of power.

ARE ART AND CULTURE synonymous? Are you automatically cultured because you can create great art?

I am not sure. Dante wrote super poetry, but was he cultured? It is fortunate that no one reads the whole of Dante in India. I got a brief look at him at university and returned to his work at greater length only during my researches on the conflicts between Muslims and Christians. Anyone who has read Dante on the Prophet of Islam and on Islamic icons like Hazrat Ali will know that Salman Rushdie has been banned for much less. Dante is vicious. Can a bigot be cultured? I think not.

FLORENCE IS OVERWHELMING EVEN when glimpsed briefly. I have seen nothing and yet after a visit to the New Sacristy of the Medici Chapel it seems as if I have seen everything and must pause before I return to see more. Michelangelo's elegy to time in four statues is a pinnacle of human achievement. Lorenzo II died without a male heir at the age of 27, of tuberculosis and syphilis, symbol of the decay that killed the most colourful and eponymous dynasty of Italy, the family that made Florence both a Jerusalem of art and a Babylon of sin. The artist was commenting on an age that had disappeared, on a family that he loved and on his own age, for he was in his 50s now and tired ('If I work one day, I need four to rest' said the man who when inspired used to work with minimum sleep and less food). During the 14 years he spent on the chapel, he lost his father, his favourite brother, his bastard-stepbrother, Pope Leo X, the Medici dynasty, and, to raise the ante, witnessed the plagues of 1522 and 1527.

Time is defined by four images: Dawn is a woman, with restless eyes, her body half asleep from the night and half-thrusting for the promise of the day. Beside her is Dusk, a man with a fading face, whose tired body heaves as it seeks rest from the labours of the day: you can see the marble body heave gently and the illusion becomes the reality. Across the sacristy are Day and Night. Day is a powerful man whose face has been left deliberately incomplete, an impressionist series of chiselled notches and whose limbs twist in myriad directions as he rests against one powerful arm draped behind his back. Night is beautiful, a gentle woman who sleeps in supple strength, a shimmer with a crescent moon on her forehead, an owl under her knee, and poppies under her feet. Michelangelo wrote this verse on sleep:

As long as shame and sorrow exist
I'd rather not see or hear
So speak softly and let me sleep.

Beside Sleep lies a mask, at first sight demonic. But look intently at that mask, and it forms a face. Is that the signature of Michelangelo lying beside Sleep?

7

8 MAY 2005

A PROVENCE DIARY

Do good food and good news taste better when touched by enchanting style and environment? Such questions of high philosophy seem inevitable after a few days in the south of France alias Provence. We are tucked into the first slope above the Mediterranean. Sunset is ahead, the sea behind, and the breeze pampers us from all directions. We overlook the serene village of Valbonne, which, despite its anonymity, boasts of a one-star Michelin restaurant. The village has a modern town hall, ancient streets, a large pharmacy, a modest parking lot and an internet cafe that opens 15 minutes late but is managed with visible sincerity by a young man in constant need of conversation. A swerve of the road later is Mougins, where the chef Alain Llorca offers a three-star Michelin meal and where Picasso came to die. The chateau, which was his last home, sits quietly with its memories. Inevitably, the locals say that the unique natural light of these mountains drew the painter like a magnet and to see the spreading blush above the kohl-black mountains long after sunset is to understand why 'silhouette' is a French word.

Michelin's stars are more respected by the discerning than its tyres, although the tyres pay for the dilettantes who wander incognito through France checking the quality of levels of the nation's highest art form, gastronomy. Fewer are aware of what the stars indicate. A restaurant can get only three at best. One star means excellent food. Two indicate that the restaurant is worth a detour. Three stars insist that the restaurant is worth a journey.

IN FRONT OF US rise the Alps, the highest peaks still glittering with the glowing white glamour of winter. Behind us is the pearl necklace of fairytale beach-towns from St Tropez to Monaco through Cannes, Antibes and Nice. The chances of seeing a pram are much higher in the touristy afternoons of St Tropez than a bikini. The place is much too expensive for the young and the beach too public for the rich and famous who remain rich because of their accountants and famous because they stay at home unless summoned by the camera. There is a traffic jam of boats on the shore and villas on the shoreline. Boat to bungalow is via a Bentley. Nudists have the privilege of their own offshore island where you cannot wear clothes even when strolling with a trolley through the foodstore. There is no equality like nudity, which is one more reason for the rich to leave such options alone. And voyeurs must find such freedom simply too boring.

CANNES POUTS AND WAITS for its suitors. They come in all shapes, from all directions, enjoy a flirt and return home. Nothing more is expected, nothing more is delivered. Cannes is a strip of four parallel curvaceous lines between sea and mountain: beach, promenade, shops and exit route. The beach is the altar where the sun god is worshipped. Celebrities receive their homage on the promenade with its majestic hotels, paparazzi and throngs of hangers-on. The pantheon of the gods of fashion dwells on the shopping street, the Rue de Antibes. Common sense presides over the exit highway: there is only so much that you can take. The sea is saucer-calm all along the coast, but water is incidental to its joys. The true deity is the sun, demanding its daily sacrifice of skin and burn from men and women who flock in from the cold, wet, grey, dismal, depressing, dull, driven regions of north Europe. The coast sparkles with dream towns till Monaco where it swerves south into the upper thigh of Italy, as beautiful a resting place for a tired head as any in the world.

IF MUSIC IS THE food of love for Shakespeare then food is the music of love in Provence. To eat such food in a hurry would be a high crime. To expect such food elsewhere would be a misdemeanour. To return to our opening query: is pleasure enhanced by environment? Yes. It's like love. Looks are not essential; but they always help. Taste buds need nature's embrace to flower.

Eze is a twelfth century village atop an ageless hill perpendicular to the Cote d' Azur, towering above a sea of shifting colours. Walk the last stretch through dainty shops selling Provence jams and pottery, swing through the high gates and climb the final steps to reach the perch of the golden goat at the pinnacle. This is the Chevre d'Or, the restaurant at the heart of the four-Michelin, 33-suite chateau-hotel. (Hotels can rise above three stars.) The fuss of the waiters at the bar is the first indication that this is going to be an agreeable afternoon. The prices along the wine list suggest otherwise. The problem is quickly sorted out by the *maitre'd* who offers an excellent Provencal chilled white and hints, through various facial contortions, that all sensible guests prefer the local fare. We leave food to his safe hands and are offered the set menu. We are led, for reasons that we cannot fully comprehend but do not want to explore, to the best table with magnificent sea views. The food comes at the pace of a leisurely, sunlit summer afternoon, starting with a palate-searching aperitif that is off the menu. We meander through soup, shellfish, starters, fish, vegetables, meat, port, cheeses, two kinds of dessert, sorbet and coffee. When we rise after three hours we are consumed by the experience.

NOTE FOR TOURISTS FROM our subcontinent heading towards Provence: a brasserie in France is a kind of restaurant and not a kind of brassiere.

8

3 JULY 2005
A SANTORINI DIARY

THE CAT CAME FREE. Everything else had a price, except the view, which was priceless. The cat, brown-grey with blue eyes, Ottoman whiskers, sat upright on the white stone wall, her body silhouetted half against a blue sky and half against a blue sea and checked me out impassively. Satisfied with what she saw or tempted by the breakfast on the table of my neighbour across the wall at the Canaves Oia resort, she scurried off, leaving nothing between me and a horizon indistinguishable from the sea.

Canaves is an exquisite series of terraced rooms set up on a cliff rising above the Aegean, on the island of Santorini, the diamond in a cluster of thousands of jewels collectively known as the Cyclades. Its special claim to fame is that it is volcanic, the last eruption being in 1939. But the Big Bang came in BC 1500. The truth is buried in legend; the line between the two is in any case delicate in a land with as much history as Greece. The Athenian statesman Solon (sixth century BC) made the first recorded suggestion that this Santorini-based volcano-cum-tsunami sent the fabled city of Atlantis to the bottom of the ocean. Since then it has been settled/ruled by a circle of neighbours, all of whom took their turn: Phoenicians (today's Lebanese), Spartans, Egyptians (under the Ptolemys), Byzantines and Ottomans until Greece won her independence in 1821. The past appears in the most unexpected forms: the Ottomans are visible in a local variation of the *shalwar-kameez,* still worn by a few middle-aged women in an era of tops and jeans.

YOU KNOW YOU ARE ageing when your head gets fried.

When we cruised around the volcano I was ready to believe every story told in every folk song about these magical waters, of mermaids and demons and ghosts and sailors enchanted into stone in mysterious caves inside a sea of heavenly blue. (It is heavenly; water is colourless, and adopts the hue of the sky.) Our gentle timber boat might have been from the past as well, except for the motor and the absence of sails. I kept wondering why it seemed familiar, since my sole previous trip to Greece had been restricted to Athens and a ride to the oracle at Delphi, until it struck me that I might have seen something similar in *The Guns of Navarone*. Gregory Peck was not around, but I did espy a couple of Anthony Quinns. My fellow guests, unmindful of age, were happy to plunge into the cool waters when we rested under the shade of a volcano. I remained on deck, in shirt and trousers, not out of modesty, but inability and caution. I can't swim and have no appetite for sunburn. I appreciate the desire of the white person to turn brown, a much better colour, but we are already there. Back on shore it took me time to understand the slight scratchy itch on my head. I had forgotten to wear a cap, because I had forgotten I was bald. My scalp now looks like a map of the world with more than five continents, and I can't even hide it with hair.

WE WERE IN GREECE for the annual conference of the *New York Times*' worldwide partners and in Santorini as the weekend guests of Themis Alafouzos, scion of a great Greek family and owner of a great newspaper, *Kathemirini*. I have rarely met anyone as gracious and charming as his mother. Pearls of a dazzle I have never seen, nor am likely to see, might have set her apart at first glance, but as a hostess she was in and out of the kitchen of the Katina taverna on the seaside, personally supervising the food and then attending to each guest with elegance and charm. A gang of newspaper managers and editors can be as cynical as any lot in the world, but we melted: everyone wanted a picture with her. At one point she turned to me, her voice full of paternal censure, looked disdainfully at my robust cigar and asked, 'Why do you smoke?' All potential wisecracks about helping Comrade Castro's economy froze on my lips. I meekly put the cigar away, delighted to experience schoolboy guilt after decades.

SOCIALISM IS ALIVE AND well in Santorini. You can hire a donkey from the capital, Fira, to the old port, Yialos, for three euros, or take the quaintly named Funicular for two. The latter takes only five minutes for the journey, but if you are counting minutes, don't go to Santorini. The Funicular was a gift to the island from a certain Evangelos Nomicos, but not before the trade union of donkey drivers had made its point: 20 per cent of the gross receipts (gross, not net) from the Funicular go to the Fira Union of Mule Drivers. The trade union lives! So does Communism, which gets about eight per cent of the vote in every election. The spirit extends beyond the eight per cent. The graffiti in Athens attests to a strong tradition of anti-imperialism. Some of the graffiti about George W. Bush and Osama bin Laden in a quiet street just below the Acropolis cannot be printed. It would get me into trouble with America's Homeland Security.

THERE IS AN INCIDENTAL, but entertaining, connection between Greece and the George Bush presidency. About two years before Bush was first elected, a small group of intellectual-activists sat down to fashion the agenda that could bring him to power (Condoleezza Rice is the starring survivor of that group). They called themselves the Vulcans after the Graeco-Roman god. As is well-known, the Romans absorbed the Greek pantheon into their worship and gave them Roman names. And so Ares, the god of war, became Mars, Aphrodite became Venus and Hephaestus became Vulcan. It has been wisely noted that the ancient Greeks did not have a religion; they turned their fears into gods and then made the gods behave like themselves. *The Odyssey* narrates the story of how Hephaestus (Vulcan) trapped his wife, Aphrodite (Venus), when she was making love to Ares (Mars) by ensnaring them in his net.

Why on earth did George Bush's intellectual mentors name their group after a cuckold? And what happens when a Vulcan tries to emulate his wife's lover, Mars? Is this an explanation for the misadventure known as the Iraq War?

IF THE GREEKS UNDERSTOOD war, their dramatists also understood the futility of it and no one better that Aristophanes who wrote *Lysistrata* in BC 411. She found the perfect solution to the bitter and unending wars between Athens and Sparta, who continued to fight even when the hated enemy, the Medes (today's Persians), were at their door.

Lysistrata organised what might be called the first women's trade union and struck work in a unique way. They decided to deny their men sex until the Athenians and Spartans had stopped fighting. The oath that Lysistrata made the women take is worth repeating: 'I will not allow either boyfriend or husband to approach me in erect condition. I will live at home without sexual activity. I will not raise my legs towards the ceiling...' and so on.

Lysistrata won the day by shutting down the night. Anyone, incidentally, who thinks boyfriends are a modern idea should read the ancient Greeks.

IT WAS NOT ONLY LYSISTRATA who saved the Greeks from speaking Persian. The oracle at Delphi, which was always consulted before any great event, played its part as well. When Xerxes threatened to overwhelm Athens in BC 480 the oracle advised Athenians to put their 'trust in the wooden walls'. The general interpretation was to take a stand behind the city walls, but Thermistocles argued that the wooden walls meant their ships made of wood. And so Athens challenged Persia on the sea and won the historic battle of Salamis. The oracle succeeded because, like an Indian astrologer, it left more than one option open.

I OFTEN WONDER WHY GREECE is hyphenated with western civilisation when it is so eastern. At the airport immigration counter a corpulent official lounges behind another sitting at the desk. The latter is doing the work; the former, having served the nation in his prime, is preparing for retirement, which is only ten years or so away. What could be more eastern than this? On a road to the Acropolis, one municipal worker is busy repairing a drainage outlet, while three others stand around him, chatting and smoking. This is not injustice. They will work in turns, one at a time. But work together to finish the job in a quarter of the time? No chance. What could be more Indian than that?

No wonder, as I left Athens airport for Delhi, I felt I was leaving home to come home.

9

20 JANUARY 2008

A ROMAN DIARY

ROME: INDIA IS THE world's latest quotation mark. Nepal has become a question mark, Sri Lanka an oversized exclamation mark; and Bangladesh is imprisoned between brackets, the space for leeway decreasing by the day. Pakistan is teetering towards a full stop.

China has turned into yesterday's paragraph: still impressive, but with the contradictions becoming evident through cracks separating sentences.

What a wonderful feeling to be an Indian at that moment in history when the world begins to applaud as India comes within reach of that long-promised tryst with destiny and shifts imperceptibly towards the centre of the stage. The auditorium is packed with distinguished Roman faces and eager journalists. The launch of the Italian edition of my book *Blood Brothers* (published by Neri Pozza as *Fratelli di sangue*) is the excuse. They have come for another glimpse of the Indian story. The book is a portrait of the heart of India, pumping blood to its veins through valves distinct in faith but united in purpose. Italy is waking up to a question that has been asked and answered in India for a thousand years, that runs through three generations of blood brothers: how can different faiths live together? There are many convoluted answers. Here is a short one.

It takes two sides to make war. It also takes two sides to make peace.

THE WEIGHTS ON THE panel for the discussion about the book are heavy: Sandro Gozi, president of the Italian-Indian Association; Dr Roberto Colaninno, president of Gruppo Piaggio; Dr Guidalberto Guidi, president of Ducati Energia and Dr Giuseppe Marra, president of GMC. Italy's businessmen are more interested in India than Italy's politicians. That is the good news. The future is bright.

Businessmen succeed because they can read a balance sheet with bifocals. They also use night vision. They will not rev up the engines without foreknowledge of roadblocks in the night. I was asked direct questions. Let me mention two. What could sabotage India's growth? And whatever happened to Gandhi?

Honesty demanded candour. Growth would be sabotaged only if there was continued neglect of the undergrowth. Growth was incompatible with poverty, or that corrosive, besetting sin, communal violence. The reason is not virtue. Morality is important, but pragmatism is more effective. Conflict is injurious to economic growth. Mumbai can have either riots or a booming stock exchange, not both.

As for non-violence: it was a brilliant strategy against an 'invincible' empire. It is a hopeless glue for a nation state. The state cannot turn the other cheek against secession or terrorism.

ONE SHOULD HAVE EXPECTED the favourite question of TV, print and radio journalists. What is common between Italy and India? I can think of two attributes immediately. Both Italian and Indian men are in love with, and in awe of, their mothers. And both drive cars in the heart of the city with the imperious impatience of maniacs. The Italians have an advantage though. Don't bother if you are hit by a car in a city like Torino. The car will get hurt. The small car is not only alive and well in Italy, but has all the impishness of a brat.

ONE COULD ALSO SUGGEST a unique sense of logic common to elements of both societies. The room service waiter at the friendly, gracious and very pretty Hotel Locarno in the heart of Rome, once a boutique residence of filmstars on a Roman holiday or on Hollywood business, was irrefutable. Twice he responded to my request for a bucket of ice and soda by saying that he could not take my order because his phone was not working. The third conversation was at his initiative. He, considerately, made the call. The phone was working now, he said, with more than a hint of triumph. I wanted to check how we had managed to communicate on a variety of subjects on the two previous occasions when his phone was not working, but decided that the dialectic might be in contravention of some labour law. I decided to let sleeping telephones lie.

EVERY HUMAN BEING HAS a friend. But only a few are privileged to have a friend like Dr Pippo Marra, the large-hearted baron of a flourishing media empire. Roman doors never remain closed before him. He had the imagination to start an Arabic news service that has become a hit across the Mediterranean: Italy is divided from the Arab world by a calm sea. His company shot to international fame when Al Qaeda chose to deliver its last message through his Arabic service. A cynosure of the media, he was the architect of the generous attention that *Blood Brothers* received. He offered me the ultimate hospitality, the liberal gift of his time. The highlight of his programme for me was a football match, AS Roma versus Torino FC, at the famous Roma ground, in the second of the two encounters between the teams in the knockout Italy Cup.

If news had spread that I was going to see Romano Prodi, it might have provoked a yawn or two. When people learnt I was going to see Totti, even friends could not disguise their envy. Prodi is a mere prime minister. Francesco Totti is a genius, star of Roma and sun of Italian football.

And how that sun dazzled! He did not come on to the field till about ten minutes after halftime. Roma were still two goals in deficit from the previous game. The scoresheet was as blank as an accountant's face. Play was stopped. Totti arrived. A thunderclap from Zeus roared down from the stands. Suddenly, touch, weave and thrust shifted the dynamics of a game that had plodded down narrow furrows. Totti flicked the ball, darted across, changed position. The field became wider side-to-side and shorter goalpost-to-goalpost. The Roma midfield and front line became touched with mercury. They found the net thrice in quick succession before Torino could understand what was going on, and then banged the ball into the net a fourth time after Torino lost their will. Totti scored his 200th goal in Italian football and received a standing ovation. I expect a standing ovation from my son when I eventually receive the signed Totti shirt that Dr Marra has promised to parcel.

It is mildly reassuring to be addressed correctly. Italians call people of the Islamic faith 'Mussalmano' rather than the inelegant British 'Moslem' or the absurd 'Saracen'. Crusaders used Saracen because they thought Arabs were children of Sarah, Abraham's wife. Mecca owes its origins, however, to Hajr, Abraham's second wife. In such a fragment of language lies history. Arabs ruled Sicily till the eleventh century.

Thoughts on a literary festival in Torino. The last temptation of an author, creator of characters, is to become a character actor in front of peers. Authors tend to write from the head and speak from the imagination. Perhaps it should be the other way around, but that would be far less interesting a spectacle. A literary festival is the space between ego and alter ego. Give an author a stage and watch a peacock dance. Some do it elegantly enough. Those with borrowed plumes never stop short of the Bhangra. The best, a rare few, sit on a stone in the corner of the stage, either waiting for Godot or chuckling at themselves.

Children of the Mother Country

1

26 FEBRUARY 1995
TRAVELLER'S NOTES

LONDON: THE ONE THING you cannot get for Monday lunch at the Beefsteak Club in Leicester Square is beefsteak. But you can get Kingsley Amis and Lord Tebbit at the table, the former a glassy caricature of the famous novelist gone to monosyllabic seed, the latter looking as if he had never stopped being a Cabinet minister under the biggest bully to rule Britain since the War. By far the youngest member of this venerable institution is my host, the silver-haired and golden-tongued ex-editor of *The Observer*, Donald Trelford, who added an international dimension to his vast national fame when he briefly squired Pamela Bordes around town. That was the time when our very Indian Pamela had the editors of the two great English Sunday papers, Andrew Neil of *The Sunday Times* and Donald Trelford of *The Observer,* on a leash: one at her beck, the other at her call. Pity it didn't last; India could have had unbelievable PR.

If the English could only export tradition they would never have a trade deficit: no other race manages to preserve heritage with greater passion. The passion sits lightly, elegantly, never burdening you with its self-importance. The Beefsteak Club is a single hall that bursts upon you after two storeys of a dingy staircase whose width could not possibly accommodate some of the more generously proportioned members. At the far end a large glass window looks out on to the masses who have no idea that such an exclusive enclave exists and would be barred by two sets of high security locks if they did. A drink of champagne sits before the steward for anyone signing in to pick up; the true regulars, however, stick to whisky before lunch and house wine during it. They used to try and count the number of glasses of wine you consumed. Sensibly they have given up the practice now and simply charge everyone four glasses of it per lunch on the assumption that if you came here you could not possibly drink less.

Every club has a famous story and the Beefsteak reminds first-time visitors about the time when three members reached the street after a decent dinner. A zealous member of the constabulary, charged with keeping that area of Soho safe, confronted the three gentlemen and asked them who they were. The foreign secretary, replied the first. The cabinet secretary, said the second. With all the sarcasm at his command the policeman turned to the third and said, 'And you, I presume, must be the Archbishop of Canterbury.' 'As a matter of fact,' came the weighted reply, 'I am.'

It is not recorded if these three gentlemen drank as much or as silently as Kingsley Amis in dotage. The conversation at the long, single table was proper lunchtime ruling class, sticking to the obvious in subject and unusual in content: Oxford (up there in '53? Ah, '57. Was John still Master of Sellwyn?); the prime minister (still a bit of doubt about whether he was finished or not; they generally thought not); cricket (we need Bangladesh; we have to have a country we can still defeat); and Islam (why didn't the Ottoman Empire improve the range and mobility of its guns? Europe could have been had for the asking). A comment on Iran by my new friend, the chairman of the Broadcasting Standards Authority, drew a sharp gasp from a younger (that is, about 60) member across the table: 'Forsooth, sir, forsooth!'

The English are different from you and me. They have more clubs.

THE ENGLISH CONTINUE TO feel very pleased about the progress of English, the language. Who can argue? Any nation which can produce both Shakespeare and Adam Smith is bound to retain control of history long after it has lost out on the geography.

Adam Smith, a good Scotsman, structured the economic thinking of the Empire-builders, while Englishmen like Burke and Macaulay scripted the grammar of political behaviour. The coincidental triumph of democracy, capitalism and the English language is the lasting hurrah of the British Empire. It would be foolish to assume that the legacy is going to be safe with the Americans. First, their relationship with the English language is at best tenuous. Second, while greed is an understandable engine of progress, it is not the same thing as narrow-band vision. One often feels that American capitalism has not thought its way through. And the political grammar of the American empire is far too flexible, too event-oriented and result-influenced. Policy cannot become a victim of a four-year cycle of presidential elections. The English have lost out elsewhere, but they do their best to keep a leonine eye on their language.

2

10 DECEMBER 1995

PAGAN CHRISTMAS: A LONDON DIARY

CHRISTMAS IS FAR MORE popular in pagan England than Christ. One reason might be that the Lord has not been backed by a good advertising campaign in this century, while Christmas is nothing if not one long, uninterrupted jingle. In the old days it was different: nineteenth century table-thumpers made sure that the fear of God was a constant on the emotional horizon of the masses. Alas, the only thing that evokes similar dread amid the citizenry in the twentieth century is taxes. If the spirit of giving has survived the oft-lamented death of belief, then much of the credit should really go to the credit card. But fie! Scepticism is an even worse disease than consumerism and the sparkling, clean-triangle trees on both pavements of Oxford Street do have a nonchalance of their own, however cardboard their branches might be. The shops are bubbling over with unfamiliar values like courtesy and attention; competition ensures that much. For all the alleged variety of the free market there is a great sameness about what is on offer: this Christmas even the relief of a mechanical Japanese novelty promoted into a fad is missing.

The only change is in the air. For the last five years, London has not only been experiencing an Indian summer but also an Indian winter. Sweat and heat in August and rain and bluster in winter. The younger generation is in serious danger of forgetting how white a

White Christmas could be. This year is different. Ladbroke's, which takes bets on both man and beast, has dropped the odds from 5-1 to 2-1 after a £3,500 flutter by a punter on the colour of 25 December this year. The signs are promising. The first snowstorm of the season arrived last Tuesday blowing in from Siberia, which is about as authentic as you can get when it comes to snowstorms. An imperious frozen trickle developed across Queen Victoria's frown on the famous statue in front of Buckingham Palace, while the unicorns on the famous gates seemed startled at having greyed overnight. White lines crawled along the bare arms of the trees in Hyde Park and a bitter wind laced the deceitfully gentle drift of grey specks from an unremitting sky. The sleet-slick, fog-heavy streets were clogged with cars moving at a foot a minute and the airwaves were jammed with complaints about local councils completely unprepared for the snow. For a country as obsessed with weather as is Britain, the lack of preparation was remarkable. It was as if India had been surprised by the monsoons.

Much to everyone's relief, matters returned to normal by Friday. An old lady, who till that time had not been able to afford a proper bowl of soup every day, won ten million pounds in the national lottery, leading to a spate of stern articles on how to protect cash from suddenly loving relatives. And the sun reappeared.

In London, the winter sun drops by for lunch. It takes care not to do so too often; you can so easily outstay your welcome with the British. But once or twice a week, it appears, smart and friendly, around opening time at the pubs, circa eleven, and fades around three in the afternoon after a pleasant frolic, leaving enough opportunity for night to set in by four. This happy – if literally lukewarm – intervention is sufficient for the 20-year-olds to leave their coats in the workplace and test their youth against the acid in the wind. Thought: there was life in these climates before central heating and the poor never did have the fancy fur which King Henry VIII wears in all Hollywood productions, so they must have been able to brave the cold with something less than wool.

When London purrs, it is with the silk finesse of a Persian cat. The best and the brightest have divided into two camps and if they are unequal you would not know it from the strength of their propaganda. No quarter is being given and no mercy asked either: this is war in its noblest form. Lady Diana's startling exercise in doe-eyed stiletto jabbing has split the British establishment. As a loyalist pointed out, in the old Tudor days when a wife wanted a separation instead of a divorce, she got a separation in spades; the neck used to be separated from the body. Instead of being sent to the Tower, the treasonable Diana is being feted by both John Major and Tony Blair for the very good reason that she is more popular than both of them put together. Diana is becoming so good at speeches about the despair of the homeless at housing charities that she could end up in politics.

The loyalists are concentrating on portraying Diana as a habitual homewrecker; a woman who, not content with having scalped an heir to the throne, followed her basic instinct into the life of Will Carling, the strapping captain of England's rugby team. Over asparagus soup, grilled cod and Spotted Dick (obviously a Public School dessert) at Scott's, a friend who now writes a sports column in one of the great dailies told me of a dinner at which Carling was also present. In the mid of the festivities he was summoned to the phone. He returned to the table wearing a slightly flushed look and announced, 'SHE WANTS ME. NOW.'

He went.

Carling's marriage has broken up. But Diana loyalists are not taking it lying down, if the phrase is appropriate. Charles himself is being spared since his upper lip is currently stiffer than any other part of his body, but his cohorts are being ruthlessly hunted down. The biggest, including physically, target is the present minister for defence, Nicholas Soames, heir to a great name and chum of Charles who sat in on the *Panorama* interview where Diana dabbed her eyes and spoke enough of the truth to make the Palace bleed. Like a typical contemporary Tory who can be trusted to do the wrong thing for the right reason, Soames went after Diana on television with the energy of a suffering bull, prompting the prime minister to distance the government from his views at the earliest opportunity. Women, who have rallied to Diana's cause, are targeting the 16-stone Soames. The story is repeated, amid great cheering, of an ex-girlfriend of Nicholas Soames who described what lovemaking with him was like – like having a wardrobe fall on you, with the key sticking out.

The wisest comment on the civil war that I heard was simple enough: 'You see the face of the 19-year-old virgin who married

Charles and see the face of the mother of the future King now ... who can blame Diana for taking revenge against those who changed her into this!'

TAILPIECE: GUESS HOW MUCH PROFIT RUPERT MURDOCH MADE FROM HIS London companies last year. £759 million. Guess how much he paid in income tax. You are right. Nothing.

3

27 SEPTEMBER 1998

A SEASON OF MIST AND MELLOW FRUITFULNESS

Autumn is a cross-dresser. It sleeps with summer in the afternoon and flirts with winter at night after playing with dusk all evening. But such is its gentle embrace that this trigamy works.

We reached England about two hours after reaching Heathrow. London is often confused with England. The English also live in London but they are only one of the communities which inhabit a true world-city. Heathrow is a terminal in every sense of the word. This is the end of the rainbow for millions of ambitions and if the pub at the end of the rainbow is not quite filled with gold it is still immensely more attractive than the dross back home. The airport smells of the world: in the advertisements for St Lucia lighting up the long route to immigration ('one-way ticket also available'); in the faces of the shops, brown and Chinese and Balkan; in the languages that whisper from the bag-and-children-strewn lounge; the hum that hovers over the restaurants and news-stands; in the bustle of the perfume counters and whisky rows at the duty free shops; and in the startling mix of eyes that meet a single sweep across this contained horizon. It is not only poverty and need that drive people to this city. London is now the financial capital of the world, thanks to Margaret Thatcher, who gave back Hong Kong to China's snares and converted London into a suitable alternative. London is the clearing house of most of the world's paperwork, for the law of England makes it the anchor of world trade and negotiation. London is not owned by the English. It is owned by the gnomes who once lived in Zurich or Hong Kong or Kenya or Mumbai and now only return home for holidays.

THE ENGLISH LIVE OUTSIDE and watch you with bemused smiles as you spend an evening in the Mariner at Windermere in the heart of the Lake District.

We drove through a season of mist and mellow fruitfulness; the last of summer's abundance in the trees, as man, animal and nature unconsciously prepared for the dark months of wet and bitter cold. We crossed the industrial heartland, through the cities that have become synonymous with the greatest football clubs of the world. When Rupert Murdoch bought Manchester United for a billion pounds, he was not purchasing 11 players and a coach. He was acquiring a brand name which would add value to almost every element of his media empire across the world. It already has.

The factories and constipated traffic jams open up to Robin Hood country, and to Warwickshire, and the jewel at its centre: Stratford-on-Avon, where Shakespeare was born and where his genius gave birth to incomparable literature. Shakespeare was a genius without being a snob. He gave us both Macbeth and Malvolio. The latter was convinced and therefore comic; the former uncertain and therefore tragic. The poet wandered through the space in between.

The Lake District was the home of the House of Lancaster and a sky as red as the rose welcomed us as we drove into the hills above the lakes. To the east is York: less romantic and more victorious. Why do the cavaliers always lose? Possibly because they are cavalier.

ALL GOOD JOURNEYS IN England must, of near necessity, end in Fawlty Towers. There are two points about the most famous television hotel in the world which are generally overlooked. The first is that Fawlty Towers is not fiction. It is bare-bones real life. I now believe that the British Tourism Authority sanctioned the funds for this series and that it is a documentary. Only the truth, the full truth, and nothing but the truth could be so funny. The second point is that the humour owes as much to the guests as to Mr and Mrs Fawlty.

Our version of Fawlty Towers was called the Biskey Howe Villa Hotel. The word is Biskey and not a typo for Whiskey. Its resident proprietor, John Candy, wears an apron, says good morning each time you see him, serves at the bar and cooks in the kitchen while a lady who is not sure about the telephone number of the hotel does the rest of the work. I am not too sure that she is Mrs Proprietor; Mrs Proprietor could be out playing bridge with her friends at the Windermere Club. There is also a fax machine in the hotel, but not actually in the hotel, if you see what I mean. Mr Candy has to bring it from somewhere when I need to use it. Mr Candy looks content. At the rates he is charging he has every reason to be happy.

4

4 OCTOBER 1998
A PICTURE POSTCARD, SLIGHTLY DAMP

GOD WAS DISCUSSING THIS new concept. He wanted Earth as the centre of His universe, where he would relocate a couple of His problem children, Adam and Eve. And the finest place on Earth, He said, would be a country called Scotland. The mountains would teem with forest and game; the valleys would be fertile with crops and flowers; the rivers would be filled with salmon and trout; and the water would be so magical that if you mixed it with barley, it would in the fullness of time turn into an elixir called whisky. Gabriel, a thoughtful sort of angel, interrupted the Almighty. Wasn't, he wondered, God getting a bit too partial to the Scots? 'Not really,' replied the Almighty. 'You don't know what kind of neighbours they are going to get.'

It is this sort of humour in the Highlands that is breeding a dangerous new phenomenon: English nationalism.

TAMDHU IS NOT THE opening chant of a Buddhist mantra. It is the first cousin of Cardhu and a good friend of Lochdhu. *Dhu* means rock; loch is a lake, as any student of the Loch Ness monster knows; *car* means black. It might however confuse you to learn that Lochdhu is black, and Cardhu golden, withTamdhu poised, colourwise, somewhere in between. They are all single malt whiskies, largely because there is nothing called a double malt or a treble malt. There are either single malts or blends like Johnnie Walker, made by a master-blender who selects the right proportions of different malts to give the marketing people something to talk about. Cardhu retains a special place in local affections because it is the only whisky created by a woman bootlegger. Her name was Helen Cumming and she joined Johnnie Walker in 1893 to provide the base for the world's most famous brand.

SCOTLAND IS A PICTURE postcard dampened by rain. English friends have taken a troubled view of our decision to spend a week under an umbrella and describe it as a holiday. It is difficult to make them understand that if we were anxious for sunshine we would have stayed back in Delhi. We are delighted to report that the sun has disturbed us with its presence for only one day in seven. Nor should we confuse this rain with monsoon; it is an intermittent drizzle, as if the permanently perched, heavy cloud needed relief from a sated, upturned bowl. But that is the only cliché which is true. The other qualities commonly attributed to Scots, of being dour and stingy, are libels. They are careful with both their money and their humour, it is true, but that is because they do not want to waste either. The air of gloom – a literal fact – has been accentuated by the Calvinist reputation of the Church of Scotland, but the pubs, which are far more crowded than the churches, permeate a convivial warmth that closes each day on a perfect note.

ENGLISH SPOKEN HERE, SAYS a message at Cairngorm Hotel in Aviemore. The Scots don't actually speak Scottish; they keep the language alive primarily to irritate their neighbours, who have so successfully turned English into the world's most effective communication highway. Read a map to learn that this is another nation: Lairg, Brora, Golspie, Dornoch, Tain, Bantt, Fochabers, Craigellachie, Aberlour, Drumnadrochit, Beaully, Dingwall, Braemar, Aboyne, Banchory, Dalwhinnie, Pitlochry. If such a litany is interrupted by Fort Augustus and Fort William it is only evidence of the English conquest; these were the havens from where they ruled before they realised that the cost of ruling the Highlands was higher than the cost of leaving them alone. There is now a new invasion underway, from an insidious and unsuspected enemy: the Bangladeshi restaurant selling Indian food. Every small town has a place offering subcontinental food under a heavily polluted brand name called tandoori and a more appropriate sub-brand called balti. No one inside these places has ever been introduced to a tandoor, but the food certainly seems to have been cooked in a bucket borrowed from a bathroom. We ventured into one of these spots, in Pitlochry, called Prince of India and tenanted by young Bangladeshi men who had taken effective training as thugs and possibly supplemented their income by a little winking on the side. An army, Napoleon famously said, marches on its stomach. In the case of Bangla curry-shops in Scotland, the stomach marches through an army.

YOU PAY ONLY £8 per head to find out that the Loch Ness monster is a well-organised scam. St Columba apparently saw something in the dark waters of the Loch Ness in the sixth century; but no one mentioned it again until 1933 when a new road was built from Inverness to the Urquhart Castle, a twelfth century pile now in ruins and tourists from America began to arrive, closely followed by journalists. Various sightings were recorded with a regularity achieved by extra-terrestrial aliens. The 'monster' began to look like an eel which had over-indulged on either Lochdhu or Cardhu. Now that the Japanese are also at the Loch Ness, fully armed with cameras, a lifesize model of this hallucination has been placed outside the local hotel. The captain of the small boat which gives us a spin on the water says that he did see a monster once, blinked, shook his head and found it was a red deer swimming across the breadth of the loch. It seems that the mysteries of this lake are far more interesting than an oversized eel: for instance, the temperature of the water remains a constant 6 degrees centigrade even when it is 29 degrees below zero all around. The water never freezes over. They have also discovered fallout from the Chernobyl nuclear disaster in the sediment. But who would spend eight pounds to hear a classroom lecture? The truth is too pious to be saleable. There is nothing like a lie to fetch eight pounds.

THEY PROTECT CAWDOR CASTLE with a white lie; no one tells you that Macbeth, the most famous Thane of Cawdor, never actually lived here. The motto of the family is the only hint: 'Be Mindful'. Good suggestion. The Macbeth action was set elsewhere, at Glamis Castle, between Perth and Aberdeen. But across the street from where we are based in Aviemore is a small and strange grassy knoll, marked by a circle of jagged white stones planted into the soft earth, and now protected by the Scottish heritage trust. Sacrifice was offered here. Of course. This was the road Macbeth took to Cawdor, through the wild mountains of Aviemore, through thunder, lightning and rain across the dark heath when he beheld the three witches and asked the fatal questions. Never ask about your future. It may come true.

5

23 APRIL 2006

A TOAST TO YOUR MAJESTY

It's Friday, 21 April 2006 in England, the sun is jesting with the rain and a faint chant rises from the television screen: 'Two ... four ... six ... eight ... who do we appreciate? The Queen!' It is Queen Elizabeth II's 80th birthday and we are all children now, staring at Windsor Castle.

Sky News, the tough TV channel, has an 'exclusive' interview with the Queen's younger son, Andrew, the Duke of York, and he takes us to an exclusive tour of the mailbox he made when he was nine, and which has been preserved, possibly because it was the most useful thing he has done. A man wearing a paper Union Jack hat tells us breathlessly that he has spoken to the Queen for the 114th time since 1982. He must be the royal version of the English cricket team's Barmy Army. A schoolgirl who offered flowers to her monarch reveals, once again exclusively, what the Queen told her: 'Are they from the garden?' Even the child sensed that there might be something less than adequate in the quote. 'And that's all,' she added.

The Queen's minders were politically correct. Once upon a time, many history books ago, the monarch of Great Britain had all the colours of the world among her subjects. The Queen of Britain still has all the colours of the world among her subjects but they all live in England instead of across the globe. The sun definitely sets upon the British Empire these days. A black girl in a pretty frock curtseys and presents flowers; children of South Asian origin, on holiday from school, line up among the 20,000 or so who have come to cheer their queen. There are gun salutes at the Queen's various residences. Since we see them on the small screen, there is a feel of toy guns on doll grass booming across Lego ramparts.

Prince Charles, who has been teased by the cartoonists in the morning papers as the long-suffering heir of the Eternal Mother, pays an impressive tribute, but the theme is mother rather than queen, reinforcing the maternal and bringing the Queen into every mother's heart. He recalls the child who waited anxiously for mama's phone calls from exotic countries, a crackle travelling at pre-computer pace and a Marconi tremble. He mentions a vignette: before her coronation Queen Elizabeth tried on her crown to check its weight and size. One doesn't want to be surprised, even by a crown.

It's sycophancy, but it is endearing and it works. There is no logic to it, but that is obviously its strength. Does the British monarchy work precisely because it is powerless? Yes, of course. People cannot hate anyone without power and the British royal family wisely edged away from politics before it could become politics' victim. Instead of power, it has influence and it would be foolish to underestimate the depth of this influence.

If only someone could convey this simple fact to the foolish man who pretends to be a king in Kathmandu.

WE DISCUSSED THE MYSTERIES of the charisma over a jolly lunch at a Scottish fish restaurant across the Fitzwilliam Museum in Cambridge. My friend of thirty years, Alexander, was dressed with the careful scruffiness of the British upper class. His elder brother John, who is 78, buys rare books from the widows of Cambridge dons as a hobby and sells them for a modest living, offered a loyal toast. John then explained how to recognise a voice on the telephone that had been outsourced to Bangalore. It was the only one, he pointed out, with a proper upper class British accent.

Last week Alexander was at the funeral of Lady Heskett, widowed at 25, but lived to a grand old age as owner of one of the greatest homes in Britain. Nigel Lawson, former Chancellor of the Exchequer, gave the funeral oration and told a charming anecdote.

When Edward Heath, a bachelor, became prime minister, he often asked grand Conservative ladies to be official hostess at his weekend retreat when he had important guests. Mrs Indira Gandhi had come to dine at Chequers and was being very critical of the British Raj. When

Lady Heskett, her hostess, could take it no more, she pointed out that there was at least one thing that Mrs Gandhi could be deeply thankful to the British for. What was that, asked Mrs Gandhi. 'We abolished suttee, didn't we?' said Lady Heskett.

Doubtless the conversation moved to other topics after that.

Class always wafts on wit. John wondered if I remembered the old Aga Khan, mentor of the Muslim League in pre-partition India and as rotund as wealth can make a potentate. My knowledge of the Aga Khan is theoretical, but John recalled a delegation of British Members of Parliament who went to visit India before independence. There was the usual obligatory visit to the Taj, along with intense political consultations with leaders of all parties. When the delegation returned to Britain, a reporter asked a Labour MP what had been his most memorable experience in India. 'The Aga Khan by moonlight,' replied the Labour MP.

Enough said.

My own encounter with the British monarchy has been, fortunately for me, limited. Queen Elizabeth and her German-blood consort Prince Philip were visiting India and I was one of the small crowd invited to the reception at the residence of the British High Commissioner in Delhi. Dress was formal. I wore a long silk kurta, which was about as formal as I was inclined to get in those days and since the Gurkhas at the gate didn't frown, I thought I had passed the formality test. I joined the queue to receive their majesties. Everyone got a perfunctory fleeting smile, which was nice and gracious. Prince Philip paused in front of me, took a second look at my kurta, standing out among the suits and wondered what manner of native dress I was wearing. Irresponsible by desire and irreverent by professional ethics, I suggested that the natives were in charge now, weren't they? There was steel in Prince Philip's subsequent fleeting smile.

Both Britain and the British monarchy are much improved by loss of empire. Britain is no longer in the colonies but the colonies are now in Britain. That seems fair and equitable. 'Your Majesty' is still in business. A toast to the Queen, Alexander and John, on her 80th birthday, but may it remain your majesty rather than mine.

6

8 JULY 2007

GORDON'S KNOT

LONDON: ON THE EVENING of 5 July 2007 with the unerring instinct of an ass, I missed a great opportunity to become a sycophant of the new British Prime Minister Gordon Brown. We were at the summer party of the *Spectator* in the garden of their new offices in London. There had been an unfamiliar stiffness at the entrance as invitation cards were checked, double-checked and ticked off in the manner of a functioning police station, but once inside it was again very British and very jolly. A very British fellow guest welcomed me to the Mad Mullah side of the fence upon being introduced and then described how his daughter had been converted to Islam. Apparently her maternal grandfather, a Muslim, had picked her up when she was born and whispered a prayer in her ear before he, a fulltime agnostic like most other Londoners, could do anything about it.

I escaped to the back of the garden, away from such moral dilemmas, to chat with old journalist friends, when a small gate near the hedge opened. Gordon Brown strode in without fuss and made straight for our group to greet my columnist friends. Here is what I wanted, very sincerely, to tell the new prime minister of Britain. 'May I, Prime Minister, use the opportunity of this accidental meeting to say how relieved most of us are at the quiet, efficient, unfussy manner in which you have handled the terrorist attack at Glasgow airport. You refused to make political capital out of this nasty business. You set the tone for London and your country with your calm, reminding us that "phlegmatic" is a British rather an English word. Within three days you actually reduced the threat perception level rather than pushing it up further. This may not seem very much but the rest of us, particularly in the Muslim world, have seen how your predecessor, the unsurpassed drama queen Tony Blair, flooded every television channel with his quivering lip. Blair would have probably banned all transatlantic flights from Scotland, rushed across to visit George Bush, prohibited all carry-on luggage on every plane by now even while his home secretary debated the merits of more legislation to curb British freedoms.'

In my imagination I see Gordon Brown listen intently, if modestly, to this fulsome praise, his eye lighting up only once, at the description of Blair as a drama queen, then summon the aide lurking pretty obviously two steps behind him and ask him to take my mobile number so that he can sip at the fount of my genuflecting wisdom for the rest of his decade as prime minister.

Alas, the truth is different. I was more or less a silent bystander, not because one is tightlipped by temperament, but because I had absolutely no clue to the subject they were discussing. What do the high and mighty ask a prime minister at a social gathering? It would clearly be crass to discuss policy or war. They discussed the comparative merits of 11 Downing Street, Brown's home as Chancellor of Exchequer for ten years, and 10 Downing Street, the famous official residence of British prime ministers. I know now, from the sidelines, that No. 10 has an extraordinary number of rooms behind that unassuming, even deceptively quiet facade. Had Brown actually moved in yet despite being PM for a week? No, not yet.

My cue to butt in. 'You aren't waiting until you've been properly elected, are you?' I suggested gingerly.

Over a lifetime of journalism, I have experienced my share of dirty looks. This one was brief, very brief, but unmistakeable. And a few seconds later Prime Minister Brown had moved on to a more salubrious group.

FOR THOSE WHO MIGHT miss the point, Brown is a bit touchy about the fact that he has become PM through a mechanism of the House of Commons and the Labour Party, rather than the morally proper process of a general election. Be that as it may, let it not be said that a mere, fleeting dirty look put me off my admiration.

Within a week of being in office, Brown has altered the culture of power beyond recognition. I am writing this article on 7 July, the anniversary of the horrific London bombings that left 52 dead in underground trains and shattered a nation's nerves. Brown remembered that moment with dignity and calm, recalling the pain of families who had lost their loved ones and reaffirming national resolve without stopping traffic or massaging tears. The clever manipulation of pseudo-hysteria, always carefully monitored to remain below the top rather than go over it, the continuous mobilisation of spin doctors and media hype, has suddenly vanished like a punctured bubble.

Gordon Brown used the word 'change' eight times in the short speech he made the day he became prime minister. It is already evident what he meant. It is not simply the fact that he has created a Cabinet of young people who would probably not be considered old enough to lead the youth wings of Indian political parties (the new foreign secretary is only 41 years old, and certainly got his job as much for his youth as for the fact that he was publicly critical of Tony Blair's hirsute warmongering). There is no sophisticated finger-pointing, the kind in which you never actually raise your hand in any direction but nod so heavily that one would have to be a cretin to miss the meaning. Men of Indian origin are involved in the Glasgow outrage; that is well known. But an individual's sins are not being transferred to a community or a country.

Where is Tony Blair? No one vanishes faster than yesterday's prime minister. After a decade of media dominance he is nowhere. He can be glimpsed occasionally, bland and uncertain, lost in the withering fire of drawing room jokes. But you can still gauge the success of his extraordinary media management skills. Most people in Britain remain convinced that he is the new Peace Czar of the Middle East, even though both the White House and the European Union (more gently) have clarified that peace talks are outside his mandate and that his only job is really as the new fund collector for Palestinian institutions.

GORDONIAN SOBRIETY IS CERTAINLY good governance, but does it also make for good politics? Blairite hype may be distasteful to columnists who do not have to get elected, but it won Blair and Labour three general elections. You do not argue with such a rate of success.

The answer to such a question is not available in the murky logic of an opinion or the opaque density of a government position. It can only be found through a general election. One of the finer points of British democracy draws a distinction between legality and legitimacy. Brown became prime minister through the support of Labour MPs. That is perfectly legal. But his tenure at 10 Downing Street will not become legitimate until it has been endorsed by the British electorate. It is Brown's decision as to when he takes the legitimacy test. Some are urging that he go for an election as early as in October 2007, particularly since he has a bounce that has taken Labour once again ahead of the Conservatives. That must be a hard call. When you have waited ten years to become PM you want to savour a little more of the satisfaction before risking a gamble. No matter what opinion polls might say, every politician knows that every election is a gamble.

Democracy is a huge casino. But that gamble is compulsory, not optional.

Gordon Brown will shift, in his mind and his heart, from No. 11 Downing Street to No. 10 only after the results of that gamble are known.

Wild West Mild West

1

12 APRIL 1998
A CALIFORNIA DIARY

San Francisco: What does being the richest country in the world actually mean? NASDAQ rising? Too limited. The stock exchange is a casino of professional, possessed gamblers into which a certain number of the citizenry are lured with the familiar mirage of money multiplication. Investors grow up when they eventually realise that the arithmetic of the stock exchange has much more to do with division than addition. Clean streets? You can find broad cosmetic avenues now in most parts of the world, apart from the Indian subcontinent, which preens about the twenty-first century and lives in the nineteenth. Cars? Asian cars are better. Clothes? Economic democracy has reduced everyone to the same T-shirt distributed under different brand names.

The answer is food. America smells of food and stinks of indigestion. Television would collapse without the advertisements for food and the cures for its consequences. One half of the great American economy sells food and the other half sells medicines for the after-effects. When the drug companies leave the television screen, their poorer cousins, the exercise conmen, take over. The scam is so huge that no stupidity is beyond the imagination of the health sellers. One quack, successful enough to display his wares in the middle of a popular serial like *MASH,* was telling his let-us-pay disciples that all they had to do to remain healthy was, when in office, drop a pencil on the floor and pick it up, drop it on the floor and pick it up, drop it on the floor and pick it up... Try doing that in an Indian office and you will need another job. (Except, of course, in a government job, where you could get an increment for dropping your pencil and picking it up.)

When Americans talk of a healthy economy, they mean precisely what they say. There are, broadly, two kinds of Americans. The first shows its commitment to food in folds around the navel and retreads on the chest. The second kind is absorbed almost completely in sweating out the fat that never should have reached the body in the first place. Nor is there a very defined hour for eating. This last sentence could be happily reversed: every hour is defined for eating. America would faint without hamburgers and choke with coke.

All this still does not explain why, when we checked into our hotel at eleven in the night in the very exclusive county of Sausalito after a journey from Delhi that squashed the calendar and squeezed the senses, there was nothing available to eat. 'This is San Francisco,' said our friendly receptionist. 'Everything closes at ten.' Maybe that is the other definition of wealth. Being rich means never having to delay your bedtime.

Leisure, therefore, is serious business, as was well illustrated in the *San Francisco Chronicle* the next morning. It reported that a new refrigerator had appeared on the market which did not make ice on the Sabbath. Readers will be aware that Jews are expressly forbidden by the law of the Lord from doing any work on Sabbath, the day of rest. This particular refrigerator was so Jewish it would not be surprising to learn that it had been circumcised in the factory before being sent to kosher shops.

WHAT MAKES AMERICA GREAT? A high point of capitalism must be the art of making you shell out substantial sums of money in order to frighten you to death. They do it with sustained commitment in a theme park called Great America, situated about an hour from San Francisco, on the freeway towards San Jose. It was built by Paramount, presumably during the years when its movies were bombing faster than B52s. The place is abundant with teenagers. One might have ventured to suggest that the whole idea was an excuse to hold hands, or hang together as the new terminology would have it, but in America you don't need an excuse to hang very close together. The teenagers consequently must be coming to Great America in search of horror. The biggest queue is for a ride called Top Gun. This is how you become a Top Gun in Great America. They hang you by your toes, strapped straight and upside down and then churn and twist you along the metal curves of the roller coaster at supersonic speeds. There was a genial demand from our generous host to join what he described as fun. I had to explain that this was what happened to me during my normal working hours. On my rare day off I wanted to do dramatically different things, like sitting on a park bench, staring at a beer protected in a Coke bottle, tiring myself by staring at a younger generation in the thralls of madness. However, it did occur to me that this could be good training for anyone wanting to learn the art of survival in a coalition government in India. What else are they doing to Prime Minister Atal Bihari Vajpayee, after all, except strapping him by the toes and holding him upside down in the midst of screaming infants while Ms Jayalalithaa plays fondly with the keys to the roller coaster?

SAUSALITO IS THE SOUTH of France pasted on to the south of America. On the one side is the Pacific, living up to its serene name; on the other, hills that roll through the suburban counties and the main city itself, cocooned between islands. The skyscrapers could belong to any American city. The Wells Fargo bank, a familiar of every Western, advertises its efficacy with a photograph of a coach and six horses racing through the Wild West and you half expect John Wayne to swagger through the swinging doors, a bank robber in each hand.

But tourists looking for the capital of counterculture are destined to be disappointed. Alas! The flower children have become hamburger mothers. Tourists are permitted to trundle up on a tramcar from Union Square to Fisherman's Wharf, from standard-brand shops to standard-menu restaurants, with a highly respectable Chinatown placed in between, bursting with vegetable vendors rather than pineapple bombs. Crime and private detectives have been shunted off to Los Angeles. There is excellent coffee at Buena Vista and charm at Paterson's pub but Paterson himself will tell you that the adventures of the first half of the century are history. San Francisco has, instead, become a beautiful place for those who can afford the real estate prices. There is friendship and fun in the air for those who have made it their home, the tourists are very sensibly packaged along defined parcels of territory, a sort of reserved zone for the naive, from where they can do the least damage to the locals. Open-jaw outsiders can, if they so wish, enjoy themselves with Hair Houdinis from Vidal Sassoon, the world's most hyped up barber, or pick up Victoria's Blemish Buster to improve their skins. The high point of tourist activity is a prison, Alcatraz. In its heyday it was a serial story in competitive sadism: the inmates at Alcatraz consisted of the most famous felons in the country (Al Capone etc.) and the wardens consisted of the most brutal cops in force. As your ferry sweeps past the rock on which America's most famous jail is housed, you notice some startling graffiti. INDIANS WELCOME! it screams. The racists who wrote this are talking of American Indians but that is only mild reassurance. The more relevant point is that the authorities have not bothered to remove the graffiti.

THERE IS LITTLE MORE frustrating than hearing about Sachin Tendulkar's century while in the United States, or learning that India moved from 26 for three to 301 for three in less than 30 blistering overs. It is not the distance which is the problem; the irritation comes from the fact that you cannot brag about it to anyone. There are still elements of civilisation which have not reached American shores and cricket is among them. One American, otherwise a decent, fun-filled, sane and intelligent man, interrupted a conversation about the merits of Sachin's and Azhar's centuries to ask what a wicketkeeper was. What is the point of all this education in America if cricket is not part of the curriculum? Instead Americans talk of something called a curve ball. The columnist George Will writes this week in his syndicated column that the three great achievements of nineteenth century America were judicial review, the curve ball and high school. He notes with dismay that he is extremely worried about the last of these institutions. So is this writer, but not, I suspect, for the same reasons.

THERE IS REWARD EVEN in an ethnic analysis of professional malpractice. Each year a list of doctors who have been held guilty of deceit towards their patients is published. The highest incidence of substance abuse (prescribing coke instead of aspirin) is found among white American doctors. The highest incidence of sexual abuse is found among Egyptian doctors. And the highest incidence of medical insurance fraud is found among Indian doctors. If anyone has a better story about stereotypes, do please write in.

2

21 JUNE 1998
A PUFF OF SMOKE IN CALIFORNIA

THE BIGGEST TOURIST ATTRACTION for Indians visiting the United States in 1998 is the Viagra pill. Apparently people get off the plane at JFK airport, buttonhole the male member of the welcoming party and ask for a private audience with the tablet even before they have been properly introduced to the taxi driver, in much the same manner that a previous generation made copies of *Playboy* their primary priority upon reaching decadent foreign shores. No one, of course, searches for *Playboy* anymore because *Baywatch* has made the magazine redundant. A World Banker I encountered at a yacht party in New York spent most of the conversation bewailing the Viagra enthusiasm which he had to deal with; not only did the most respectable financial analysts want to see the damn thing the moment they reach United States but they now expected him to carry it around on his world travels. He sniffed that his standard reply was that he personally did not need the stuff yet. Amen. No pill was ever sold to less and bought by more in the history of the world.

Some of the after-effects, of course, have been painful, not to the old men who are literally jumping with excitement but to the old women who are their chief victims. The old men discover that nothing comes free, not even happiness, when their backs collapse after this burst of unfamiliar exercise. Young women with sugar daddies, on the other hand, can now pretend that their daddies do a little more than put sugar into their purses. It's all happening at a fairly bewildering pace. The adultery industry, always in very good health, is booming. Is that one reason why New York hotels have become so horrendously expensive? In the pre-Viagra era (that is, a few months ago), a very good room was available for around $250 a night. Now start at $400 and keep counting. Maybe when the American economy finally enters recession again they can blame it on Viagra. Exorbitant hotel rates have already curbed business visitors from coming to New York. This, in turn, persuades them to take their business elsewhere, which affects consumer markets, which pushes up prices. Those who recall the election in which Bill Clinton defeated George H.W. Bush remember that it was the state of the economy which brought Bill Clinton to power. It would be entirely appropriate if it was Viagra which unravelled his presidency.

Poor Bill Clinton. He can appear on the lawns of the White House in front of the world's cameras to explain his visit to China, send NATO jets buzzing over Kosovo, or announce a thaw in relations with Iran and all you think about when you see his face is Monica Lewinsky. Jokes about the president and his favourite intern continue to swarm across the internet. Latest sample. A depressed businessman decides that he has had enough and returns home at three in the afternoon to find Bill Clinton lying on top of his wife. He is outraged. 'What are you doing?' he demands indignantly. The suave Clinton, never fazed, always ready with a practiced explanation, replies calmly: 'I'm listening to music.' 'What music?' roars the businessman and is immediately advised to check out. He leans over and puts his ear to his wife's breasts. 'I can't hear any music!' he screams. 'Of course you can't,' Bill Clinton replies. 'You aren't plugged in.'

THE FUTURE OF INDIA is safe. Sanctions can no longer hurt us. If the trend that has begun in California continues, India's foreign exchange earnings could make red China green with envy. Unknown to all of us, our very own *bidi* has become a cult smoke in California and once this emerging fashion becomes a rage the *bidi* will turn into the biggest dollar earner in the history of India. We owe this discovery to a survey conducted by five teenagers at the Booker T. Washington Community Center and two students at the Galileo High School, who took ten months to document a new fad they witnessed among their friends. They found that 58 per cent of the students surveyed had smoked a *bidi* at least once and two-thirds knew of someone who had tried India's genuine indigenous product. A packet of 20 *bidis* costs, according to a report in the *San Francisco Chronicle,* 'as little as $1.25

a pack'. I am certain that the *bidi* workers of India will be pleased to know that 20 of their snorters cost 'as little as' Rs 60.

The researchers also found out that the obligatory Surgeon General's warning that smoking is injurious to your health was missing on seven out of ten packs of *bidis*. What intrigues this columnist is not the seven packs on which the warning was missing but the three packs on which it was there. When was the last time that you picked up a pack of *bidis* with a health warning?

When contacted about the missing warning label, the Federal Trade Commission said that they were 'looking into it'. Let us all wish the Federal Trade Commission luck.

Sixteen-year-old Maurice Evans told the newspaper that *bidis* were available in America in strawberry, chocolate, mango and vanilla flavours to kill the harsh bite of 7 per cent nicotine. If Mr Hegde is reading this, he need not go further when it comes to choosing the top prize for export promotion awards. The report is illustrated with *bidi* packs made by Kisanlal Bastiram of Camel House, Nashik, and the brand name of this mentholated *bidi* is Kailas, with the *trimurti* as an illustration. This must be the ultimate exercise in brand equity creation. Its success was also verified by Maurice Evans. One of his friends smoked 20 packs a day, he said. 'He's addicted to them. He wouldn't listen. It went in one ear and out the other.' The Government of India should identify and invite that friend of Maurice, if only to show him what some Indians can do with a *bidi* around their ear.

IT MIGHT INTEREST YOU to know that China, which now claims a place on the high table of world affairs thanks to its bombs (built when it was poor) and its balance of payments (built out of cheap domestic labour), is still receiving loans out of the poverty fund of the World Bank. Beijing has organised for itself the best of all three worlds: First World armed power, Second World economic strength and Third World handouts. The biggest defenders of Beijing's dictatorship are heads of government across the five continents, with President Clinton leading the way as he builds up momentum for his visit to China. They used to call President Ronald Reagan the Teflon man because every crisis slipped by his office leaving him unstained. Clinton is Teflon with a poker face. The truly big scandal of his presidency has been the purchase of influence in the White House by China, but ironically, the genuine scandal has been buried by the prurient.

3

30 AUGUST 1998
HUNGRY IN AMERICA

America from a window in the night sky is geometry decorated with electricity. An arabesque of light patterns across the land makes a mockery of height; the aeroplane flying over a continent seems much closer than the 35,000 feet that, according to the friendly pilot, is where we are on this Delta flight from New York to San Francisco. The view from the window is sharper than anything sunlight might have created. The mood in the plane bustles with family-happiness; my neighbour, for instance, is going to the West Coast to spend a few days bonding with his teenage sons, clearly after having unbonded with a 50-year-old wife. In front, a Jewish father is taking five children and a content mother away from the tensions of a lucrative New York Stock Exchange. The journey from New York to San Francisco is always happier than the one in the reverse direction; the destination determines the mood. Even a two-hour delay locked in the plane, sitting on the tarmac, waiting for the excesses of Hurricane Bonnie to melt out of the clouds seemed less tiresome than it might have been after a 20-hour journey from Delhi.

Sausalito is worth the effort of the journey. It is five in the afternoon; the sun has warmed the streets to 70 degrees and the mist is peeling off sheep-coat clouds sitting on a green, tree-packed hill to my left. The bay dances to the music of sunlight on the right the rhythm punctuated by the bob of pleasure boats in a gentle wind and the swoop of birds hunting for food. The main street is lined with simple, wooden, one-floor structures. The law protects the idea of a village and permits the reality of urban luxury on the mountain slopes, where all the grand homes nudge one another for a better view. To reach my apartment I have to swivel from the high perch of the road and pick up an art deco lift that slides up at a 45 degree angle on metal tracks. The wall-size bedroom window follows a straight line down the mountain, across the street, into the harbour and beyond to a shifting horizon on the Pacific Ocean.

Friendship is the formal motto of this small town; business is its preferred activity; and it is easy to understand, once you are here, why Americans want both Monica Lewinsky and Bill Clinton, the first for entertainment and the second to run the country. America salivates at the thought of what is called in Presbyterian parlance as 'unnatural sex' in the Oval Office; but is in no mood to destroy a president who takes his pleasures seriously. Americans tolerate adultery in the White House because:

1: The lights are on all over America;

2: Macy's is offering a four-hour sale this Saturday (between 9 a.m. and 1 p.m. only) that will save the consumer an extra 40 per cent to 60 per cent on already reduced casual wear and career dresses;

3: Unemployment is down to its lowest levels in 29 years and home-construction is up to its highest levels in history;

4: The weather is gorgeous;

5: And so what? I tell lies too.

The real victims of Bill Clinton's sex life, paradoxically, could be some of his morally unstained loyalists. Vice-President Al Gore, for instance. Widely recognised as a politician with the sex life of a Sunday school teacher and the oratory of a Sunday evening pastor, Al Gore has begun to experience the first stages of premature abortion of his presidential ambitions because of a few dubious methods adopted while fund-raising for himself and Bill Clinton in the last elections. Since Americans feel good about Clinton they could well take their revenge on the hapless Gore, whose primary passion, the ozone layer, is largely outside the framework of their intellectual pursuits.

4

21 MARCH 1999

THE FALL AND RISE OF ERECTILE DYSFUNCTIONING

HERE IS THE NEWS on ABC's *Good Morning America*. It is St Patrick's Day in the counties of northern California. The Sisters of Perpetual Indulgence, who knew what they wanted when they christened themselves, have invited the wrath of the Roman Catholic Church because they want to celebrate their twentieth anniversary party on Castro Street in San Francisco on Easter Sunday. The city has given them permission, much to the outrage of the church. The 30 sisters, who are gay, lesbian, transgender and even straight, say they only want to sing, dance and promote safe sex. The church is a bit upset because they dress like nuns. In the Lake County, a commune, which grows its own marijuana, is delighted with a government report which indicates that smoking pot can be helpful to patients in extreme pain. This commune has been providing marijuana relief to unhealthy AIDS victims who are convinced that marijuana has saved their lives, while a healthy commune-manager waters the magic plant with a loving smile in indulgent view of the cameras. A male stripper has been sentenced to community service by a very stern judge for full-frontal visual service at a party of 15-year-old girls. His argument, that he was hired by the host's mother, leaves the judge unmoved. The Reverend Henry Lyons breaks down outside his Bethel Metropolitan Baptist Church after pleading guilty to swindling more than four million dollars of holy money. A new method in the treatment of breast cancer has been discovered to reduce pain: the story is shown in the *Healthy Women's Segment*, brought to you by Monistat, makers of the finest medicines in the world. The weather report, which follows, is brought to you by the makers of some dog food. The anchors shift gear to foreign affairs; we move to New York, capital of Overseas Ireland. The city is preparing to celebrate St Patrick's Day with its customary parade. The only non-American band which will play bagpipes in the parade is Japanese, according to *USA Today*. The *Wall Street Journal*, justifying its international network, reports that there is a shortage of Irish pubs in Ireland. Fortunately, there is no shortage of them in New York, or the mayor would never get elected. St Patrick, as we should know, drove all the snakes out of Ireland. Where did they all go? To television.

The husband of the woman who could become the next president of the United States is doing a television commercial for erectile dysfunction. Bob Dole, who lost the 1996 elections to a man whose erectile functioned perfectly, points out, quite legitimately, that doing this commercial required courage; it is not the sort of problem that men like to advertise. His impotence was a side-consequence of prostate cancer and he urged viewers to take this problem to their doctors rather than hide behind embarrassment. Bob Dole was unafraid to proclaim, with delighted endorsement from his wife Elizabeth, the virtues of Viagra during his own campaign for president; and he seems to have expanded the message during his wife's campaign. Is there any political undertone to this? There has to be; the Doles are seasoned political professionals. Their message seems to be about fun in marriage; Bill Clinton, in contrast, represents fun outside it, while Hillary looks like she is having no fun at all.

The Clintons look increasingly dead, both of them. A new poll shows that George H.W. Bush would have swamped Bill Clinton if the elections were held now and Hillary Clinton would lose equally badly in a Senate race to her likely opponent, New York's ebullient mayor, who cross-dresses for pantomime when he wants to have fun. There is talk that she may push for a divorce, timing it with their departure from the White House; she wants to give up her husband, not his current address. Normally presidents acquire a sort of popular glow once they leave office, defeated ones being treated more warmly than those who enjoyed eight years of glory. Clinton, who has enjoyed so much admiration as a president while in power, could become the most despised ex-president in recent American history.

VOLTAIRE, ACCORDING TO A columnist in the *New York Times*, declined a second invitation from the Marquis de Sade to an orgy with the comment: 'Once is philosophy. Twice is perversion.' Randy Cohen, styling himself as The Ethicist (a brutal deformation of a perfectly decent word), was castigating the ethics of a student who had picked up an essay from his website, offered it as her own and was now terrified of being caught and expelled by a suspicious professor; and giving advice to someone who wanted to celebrate the birthday of his friend by a tour of the topless bars in New Jersey. In the first case, Randy argued that he might have thought of helping if the student was going to be handed over to the Taliban but otherwise some salutary lesson for her low morality would be good for her. The Ethicist's posture seemed more irritating than the student's cheating, which set me thinking about Randy's morals in the use of the Voltaire quote at the end of column. It seemed straight out of a book of quotations, rather than from a study of Voltaire's life and work. No reference was given, no context to the text. From the little I have read by and about de Sade, he spent most of his life in jail. His orgies (often organised with the help of his wife) were not really public parties for the high and the mighty.

The quotation also seemed a bit glib. Why should the first experience of an orgy be philosophy and the second a perversion? Why should the first be a search for the meaning of life and the second base desire for physical pleasure? One could easily argue the case for the other way around: that the first visit was sensational and the second a more legitimate search for the nature and consequence of such sensory titillation. Did Voltaire actually say any such thing? Who translated it from the original? Or is it one of those quotations that acquires a life of its own in successive compilations of wise and witty sayings that publishers make money from? Had The Ethicist become a minor fabricator himself?

We may not be picking up entire essays from a website but we are all picking up odds to meet our ends from one source or the other. Here is some plagiarism which I am delighted to pass on to you. The hooker told the Jew, 'I'll do anything for you for fifty dollars.' 'Great,' he replied, 'paint my house.'

EVERY RELIGION IN AMERICA is big business; it must be some old-fashioned embarrassment which prevents the more successful sects and cults from being quoted on the New York Stock Exchange. Management conducts affairs on corporate principles; growth is an honourable goal and liquidity is ensured through a number of profit centres. The more colourful CEOs of these organisations ensure some special perks, as a recent judgement of a court in California confirms. Donald D. Walters, by all accounts a mild and kind man, transcended into Swami Kriyananda more than thirty years ago after reading Swami Yogananda's *Autobiography of a Swami*. Donald's search for bliss in a guru's robes has been successful. The Ananda Church of Self-Realisation, which he heads, started out as a commune occupying tents and geodesic domes, without water or electricity; its headquarters are now situated over 900 acres, it has its own schools, clinics, health-food shops, publishing wing and a phone system called Ananda Bell. It runs meditation centres as far away as Italy and Australia. You cannot fault the Swami on his levitation prowess.

Alas, Swami Kriyananda has slipped on his erectile, a popular contemporary disease made famous by Bill Clinton. He has been fined more than a million dollars for the sexual exploitation of at least six of his younger women devotees. The gullibility of these women indicated a substantial commitment to stupidity but this only made the crime worse in the eyes of the court. One victim provided details of the Swami's methods. The first step would be an invitation to clean his living quarters. Normal people try and make their first pass by inviting a lady to dinner but this is an organisation of higher learning. Cleaning the boss' bedroom was advertised in the community as an honour. The next upgrade on the honours list was an invitation to massage the Swami's back; and after she had started she was told to straddle him in order to get a firmer grip on his shoulders. An even higher honour followed. The Swami would ask the disciple to take off her clothes as the material was irritating him. In this state, the Swami helpfully added, the disciple became a 'pure channel of God'. The Swami rolled through God's channel soon enough. Senior members of the Ananda Church who self-realised that the woman might start asking questions, told her that it was 'extremely blessed to provide energy' to Swami Kriyananda and that this was 'energy going from one part of the universe to another'. With so much space travel was it any surprise that the Swami lived on such a high? He has now landed on earth and filed for bankruptcy to save a million dollars.

Mexed Missages